LEEDS PUBS

PAUL CHRYSTAL

O Yorkshire, Yorkshire: Thy Ale is so strong
That it will kill us all if we stay long:
So they agreed a Journey for to make
Into the South, some Respit there to take.

George Meriton, *The Praise of Yorkshire Ale*

I would give all of my fame for a pot of ale and safety.

William Shakespeare

First published 2020

Amberley Publishing
The Hill, Stroud
Gloucestershire, GL5 4EP

www.amberley-books.com

ISBN 978 1 4456 9688 1 (print)
ISBN 978 1 4456 9689 8 (ebook)

British Library Cataloguing in Publication Data.
A catalogue record for this book is available from the British Library.

Origination by Amberley Publishing.
Printed in the UK.

Contents

Woodhouse Cliff
Far Headingley
Woodhouse
Headingley
Armley
New Wortley
Camp
River Aire
Cunliff Wood
Museum
Fire Station
Hospital
Medical Care
Education Facility
WOODHOUSE LANE
OTLEY ROAD
CARDIGAN ROAD
ST CHAD'S DRIVE
ST CHAD'S AVENUE
BECKETT'S PARK DRIVE
BECKETT'S PARK CRESCENT
ST ANNE'S ROAD
SHAW LANE
GROVE LANE
ALMA ROAD
MOOR ROAD
HOLLIN LANE
HOLLIN ROAD
KIRKSTALL LANE
KIRKSTALL ROAD
BURLEY ROAD
CARDIGAN LANE
ST MICHAEL'S ROAD
ST MICHAEL'S LANE
BAINBRIGGE ROAD
BELLE VUE ROAD
MOORLAND ROAD
CLARENDON WAY
KENDAL LANE
HYDE TERRACE
BURLEY STREET
PARK LANE
WESTGATE
WEST STREET
WELLINGTON BRIDGE STREET
CAVENDISH STREET
ARMLEY ROAD
CANAL STREET
CASTLETON ROAD
HOLTS CREST WAY
GOTTS ROAD
GRAINGERS WAY
TONG ROAD
WELLINGTON ROAD
COPLEY HILL
OLDFIELD LANE
WHITEHALL ROAD
HOLBECK LANE
WORTLEY LANE
SWEET STREET WEST
GLOBE ROAD
WATER LANE
VIADUCT
FORGE LANE
WOODHOUSE STREET
RAGLAN ROAD
ST MARK'S ROAD
14
59
40
71
63
64
37
33/65
72
74
57
42
75
8
25
67
66
68
51/69
70
16
27
3
11
30
55
36
38

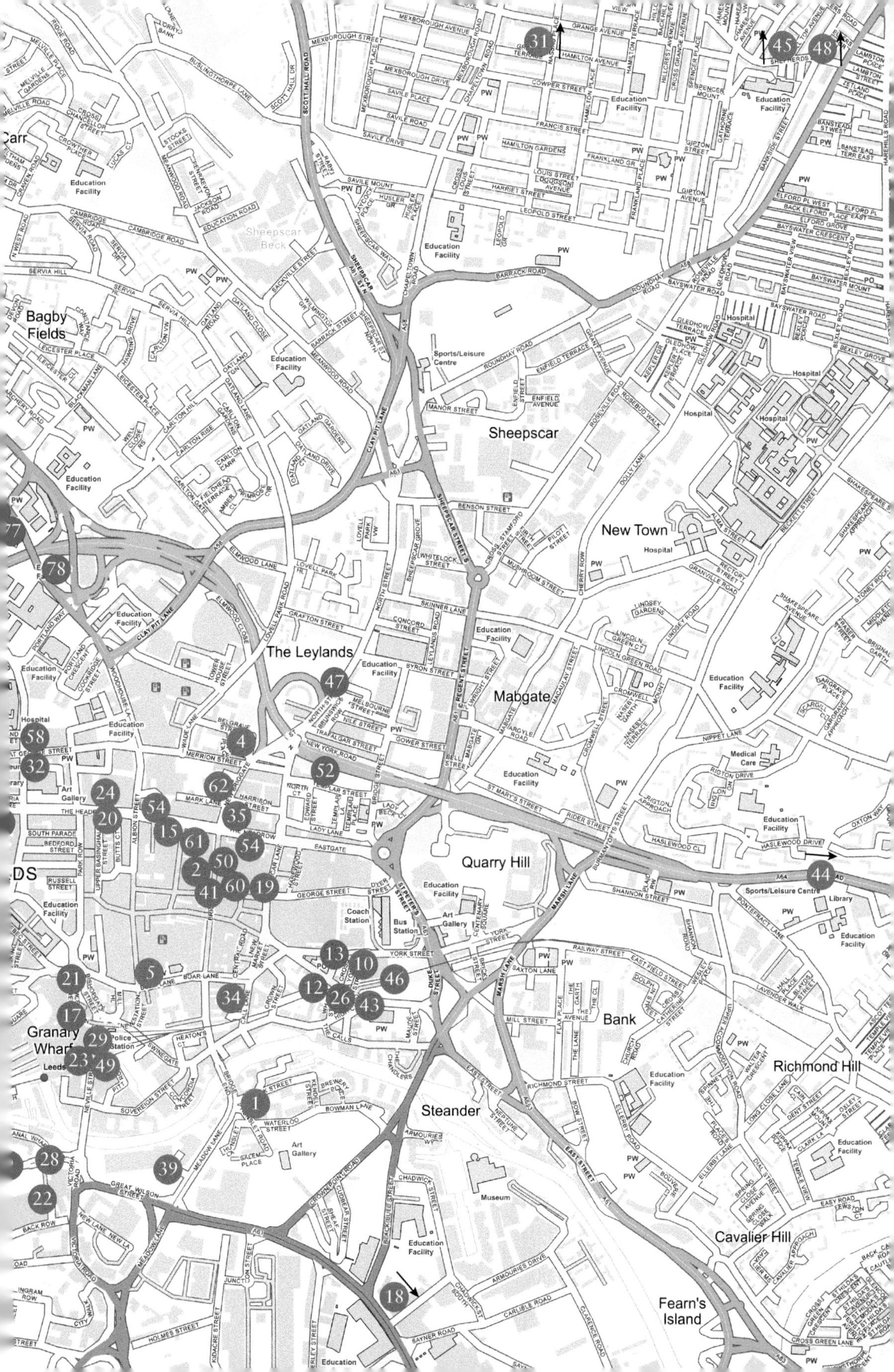
Bagby Fields
Sheepscar
New Town
The Leylands
Mabgate
Quarry Hill
Bank
Richmond Hill
Steander
Cavalier Hill
Fearn's Island
Granary Wharf
Sheepscar Beck
MEXBOROUGH AVENUE
MEXBOROUGH STREET
MEXBOROUGH PLACE
MEXBOROUGH DRIVE
SAVILE PLACE
SAVILE ROAD
SAVILE DRIVE
SAVILE MOUNT
SCOTT HALL ROAD
BUSLINGTHORPE LANE
MEANWOOD ROAD
CAMBRIDGE ROAD
EDUCATION ROAD
SERVIA HILL
OATLAND CLOSE
CHAPELTOWN ROAD
HAMILTON AVENUE
COWPER STREET
FRANCIS STREET
HAMILTON GARDENS
LOUIS STREET
HARRIET STREET
LEOPOLD STREET
BARRACK ROAD
ROUNDHAY ROAD
ENFIELD TERRACE
MANOR STREET
BAYSWATER ROAD
BAYSWATER CRESCENT
BEXLEY GROVE
CLAY PIT LANE
ELMWOOD LANE
LOVELL PARK ROAD
GRAFTON STREET
SHEEPSCAR STREET S
REGENT STREET
BENSON STREET
MUSHROOM STREET
SKINNER LANE
BYRON STREET
LINCOLN GREEN ROAD
NIPPET LANE
NEW YORK ROAD
MERRION STREET
ST MARY'S STREET
RIDER STREET
EASTGATE
GEORGE STREET
YORK STREET
BOAR LANE
SHANNON STREET
RAILWAY STREET
MARSH LANE
MILL STREET
RICHMOND STREET
EAST STREET
CROWN POINT ROAD
GREAT WILSON STREET
ARMOURIES DRIVE
CARLISLE ROAD
HOLMES STREET
PONTEFRACT LANE
SHAKESPEARE AVENUE
Education Facility
Hospital
PW
Sports/Leisure Centre
Art Gallery
Coach Station
Bus Station
Police Station
Museum
Library
Medical Care
31 45 48 77 78 47 4 52 58 32 24 20 54 15 61 62 35 2 50 41 60 19 13 10 46 12 26 43 5 21 34 17 29 23 49 1 39 28 22 18 44

Key

1. The Adelphi, Corner of Hunslet Road and Dock Street
2. The Angel Inn, Angel Inn Yard, Briggate
3. The Beech, Wortley
4. Belgrave Music Hall and Canteen
5. The Black Prince, Boar Lane
6. The Cardigan Arms, Kirkstall Road, Burley
7. The Chemic Tavern, Johnston Street
8. The Clothiers Arms, Yeadon
9. The Cross Keys, Water Lane
10. The Crowd of Favours, Harper Street
11. The Drysalters, Elland Road
12. The Duck & Drake, Kirkgate
13. The Duncan, Duncan Street
14. The Fleece, Farsley
15. Foley's Cask Alehouse, the Headrow
16. The Fox & Newt, Burley Street
17. Friends of Ham, No. 4 New Station Street
18. The Garden Gate, Hunslet
19. The General Eliott, Vicar Lane
20. The Green Dragon, also The Guildford, Guildford Street
21. The Griffin, Boar Lane
22. The Grove, Back Row, Holbeck
23. The Head of Steam, Mill Hill
24. The Horse & Trumpet, The Headrow
25. The Kirkstall Bridge
26. The Lamb & Flag, Church Row
27. Leeds Postal Service, Wellington Street
28. The Midnight Bell, Holbeck
29. The Moot Hall Arms
30. The Morley Dashers, Morley
31. The Nags Head, Chapel Allerton
32. The Nation of Shopkeepers, Cookridge Street
33. The New Inn, Headingley
34. The New Penny, Call Lane
35. The North Bar, New Briggate
36. Northern Monk Refectory, Marshall Street
37. The Old Ball, Brownberrie Lane, Horsforth
38. The Old Peacock, Elland Road
39. The Old Red Lion, Meadow Lane
40. The Old Unicorn, Bramley
41. The Pack Horse, Pack Horse Yard, off Briggate
42. The Packhorse, Woodhouse Lane
43. The Palace, Kirkgate
44. The Podger, Ninelands Lane, Garforth
45. The Preston, Roundhay Road
46. The Regent, Kirkgate
47. The Reliance, North Street
48. The Roundhay Fox, Princes Avenue
49. The Scarbrough Hotel, Bishopsgate Street
50. The Ship Inn, Ship Inn Yard, Briggate
51. The Skyrack, St Michael's Road
52. The Templar Hotel, Templar Street
53. The Three Hulats, Chapeltown
54. The Three Legs, Three Legs Inn Yard, off Lower Headrow

55. The Tommy Wass, Cleckheaton
56. The Town Hall Tavern, Westgate
57. University Refrectory, University of Leeds
58. The Victoria Family & Commercial Hotel, Great George Street
59. West End House, Abbey Road
60. Whitelock's Ale House, Turk's Head Yard
61. The White Swan, White Swan Yard
62. The Wrens Hotel, New Briggate
63. Woodies Craft Ale House
64. The Three Horseshoes
65. The New Inn
66. The Headingley Taps
67. Manahattan
68. The Box
69. The Skyrack
70. The Original Oak
71. The Hyde Park
72. The Library
73. The Packhorse
74. The Eldon
75. Leeds University Union
76. The Fenton
77. Strawbs
78. The Dry Dock

I

Opening Time

This is the fourth of my practical beer (and soft) drinker's guides – this time devoted to the public houses of Leeds. The book is 'practical' because the maps show you how to get there, I give addresses, postcodes for satnav, phone numbers and e-mails for bookings and websites (where they exist), and I point out anything special to look for, as well as the beer, once you're there. The other four books cover Hull, York, the Yorkshire Dales, and Harrogate (including Knaresborough).

As with my other books on Yorkshire pubs, *Leeds Pubs* is a bit like a good pub: accessible, friendly and rewarding with a promise of good beer. It is an engaging guide to the best pubs in the city of Leeds. The book describes in detail, and illustrates, seventy or so pubs, inns and bars still serving, plus many more which no longer exist or which have changed their use. Each pub has a unique story to tell, so, where possible, the history and development of these pubs is described with information on origins, the clientele they were built to cater for, significant events and how the pubs got their names or what the names signify, anecdotes about them and about characters who may have drunk, or got drunk, in them, and items of local interest associated with them. Join us in the world-famous Whitelock's, the Adelphi or in the Cross Keys, the Garden Gate, the Ship Inn or live at Leeds in the university union bar, in the wonderful Griffin or the Scarbrough Hotel or the Victorian Victoria Family & Commercial Hotel.

Leeds Pubs is, then, an informative and fascinating practical guide for anyone strolling in and around Leeds, one of England's most historical and diverse cities, who has a bit of time on their hands and wants to learn some local history in the most convivial of ways.

A word of caution: information is correct at time of going to press, but pubs are closing or being inflicted with a change of use all the time, so please do check the latest situation if setting out to visit.

> There is nothing which has yet been contrived by man, by which so much happiness is produced, as by a good tavern or inn.
>
> Samuel (Dr) Johnson (1709–84)

To give some historical perspective – and to highlight the seemingly inexorable decline of pub culture – back in 2003 the average pub price per pint of draught bitter was £1.95*. Times have

*www.statista.com

indeed changed: back then the average adult drank 218 pints; by 2011, that same adult downed just 152 pints, a 30 per cent drop**. In 2002 there were 60,100 pubs in the UK***. There were 50,300 pubs at the end of 2016, down from 54,194 in December 2014, according to CAMRA.

In 2009, a record number of fifty-two pubs a week closed nationally; research carried out in late 2012 by CAMRA showed that eighteen pubs were closing each week. In 1875 Yorkshire could boast some 10,000 pubs. Now there are significantly fewer, with time being called for the last time all the time. Hundreds of pubs have closed down in Leeds over the years – a disastrous 22 per cent in the ten years since 2007. Put another way, Leeds has lost twenty of its pubs in the last eight years, according to figures from the Office for National Statistics, which show that in 2010 there were 460 pubs and bars but by 2017 that had fallen to 440. Across the UK 5,745 pubs closed over the period, and there are fifty-four local authorities where thirty or more slammed the door.

Generally speaking, pubs have responded to changing drinking habits with a more eclectic offering, such as coffee and tea, zero per cent wines and beers, live music, Wi-Fi, big screen live sport, speed dating, quizzes and dining. Pubs now serve one billion meals a year and some of their chefs are among the leaders in modern British cooking. The pubs can also offer 50,000 or so bedrooms. And craft beers and the myriad microbreweries have done much to save the day and the night out. Quality, professionalism and hard work have gone through the roof, banishing forever that soapy, sloppy stuff so often ladled up in years gone by.

The message I offered in my book on the pubs of Harrogate and Knaresborough is just as valid here: 'So, if there is a message to take away from this book it is simply put the book down, get up, go out and call in at your local for a pint or two and help preserve and extend this most British of social institutions. Once the pub, your favourite pub, has gone, it's usually gone for good.'

But don't take it from me; in the words of a cautionary Hilaire Belloc (1870 –1953): 'When you have lost your inns drown your empty selves for you will have lost the last of England.'

He's right. Ask any villager whose local has been erased from the face of his main street or converted into a car park.

In the beginning pubs, particularly pubs out in the country, brewed their own ale in brewhouses next to the pub. Unsurprisingly perhaps, women did most of the work – Madam Bradley of Northallerton and Nanny Driffield of Easingwold are legends in their own brewhouses. 'Brewsters' or 'alewives' brewed ale in the home for domestic consumption and commercial sale, albeit on a small scale. These brewsters made a substantial contribution to the family income. It was good ale that attracted neighbours into their houses and led to the birth of the public house. Stingo, Knockerdown and Rumtum were famous Yorkshire brews with reputations as far south as London's Marylebone. Hopped ale was imported from Flanders around 1400, after which time hops were grown in England for beer production – ale usually has a lower hop content than beer.

At the same time hostelries were set up by the roadside catering for travellers. This had started with the Romans locating *tabernae* on their extensive road network and continued apace with merchants plying between markets, long-distance drovers, commercial travellers, monks commuting from monastery to monastery, pilgrims (as exemplified by Chaucer's *The Canterbury Tales*) and all manner of other people moving from village to village or from town to town. The

---

**www.telegraph.co.uk/finance/newsbysector/retailandconsumer/11283995/The-real-reasonsfor-the-tragic-demise-of-the-British-pub-industry.html

***www.beerandpub.com/statistics

lords of the manor sometimes provided refreshing and sustaining beerhouse facilities for the workers in their fields. Ale was an important part of the Yorkshire diet, as it was affordable and unpolluted compared to water. It is estimated that the average adult drank up to eight pints a day.

Things started to change in the seventeenth century when in 1657 turnpikes led to a huge increase in the number of horses and coaches full of passengers crisscrossing the county. Turnpikes demanded coaching inns for board and lodge for the drivers and passengers, and stabling for the horses. The railways 200 years later brought the next seismic change with the establishment of railway inns at stations. The third development was the now ubiquitous car and the transportation of goods by road, which led to a need to cater for day trippers, business people, long-distance lorry drivers and other travellers – often in the very pubs that once served coach and railway travellers.

The first common brewers were the Nesfield family of Scarborough, established in 1691. The end of the eighteenth century saw the emergence of the common brewery, which was boosted by the Beerhouse Act in 1830. Names from the nineteenth century like Hull Brewery, John Smith's, Sam Smith's, Tetley's, Timothy Taylor's and Theakston's are, more or less, still very much alive today. Beer brewing had moved out of the home and was an industry in its own right, supplying a growing number of public houses and hotels.

The Alehouse Act 1828 established a general annual licensing meeting to be held in every city, town, division, county and riding, 'for the purposes of granting licences to inns, alehouses and victualling houses to sell exciseable liquors to be drunk on the premises'. The aim of the 1830 Beerhouse Act was to encourage people to drink beer rather than spirits. Any householder who paid the poor rate could sell beer, ale or porter by buying an excise licence; they did not a need justices' licence but spirit-selling retailers did. The sellers of beer had to promise to give correct measures, maintain good order, to allow no drunkenness or gambling and not to dilute the beer! The aim was to increase competition between brewers, lowering prices. It resulted in thousands of new public houses and breweries throughout the country throwing open their doors, particularly in the rapidly expanding industrial centres of the north of England, such as Leeds. In Manchester and Salford alone there were twenty-seven breweries in 1827, increasing to seventy-five by 1873. However, not everyone warmed to the Act: many beerhouses emerged from the backstreets of large cities and became working-class drinking dens. *The Leeds Mercury* from 23 October 1830 reported, 'We receive from many quarters grievous complaints of the demoralising effects of this Act, which has, by making beer cheap, led to an increase of intoxication.'

By 1841 licences had been issued to 45,500 commercial brewers. The final remaining provisions of the Act were repealed on 11 November 1993. The passing of the Act during the reign of William IV led to many taverns and public houses being named in his honour; he remains 'the most popular monarch among pub names'.

As I remarked in the introductions to my other books on pubs in Yorkshire, in the days before satnav, if you stopped and asked a stranger the way to somewhere, anywhere, you would most likely be directed by way of the local church (if there was one) or via the local pub or pubs. Generally speaking, pubs are still, despite all the closures, the second most ubiquitous feature of most high streets, be they urban, rural or suburban. That tells you just how important pubs are to any local community; like churches, they can be the focal point of a street, estate, village, town or city centre. Like churches they can, for some, satisfy a very real need for refuge, companionship, comfort and joy.

Pub signs and the names and the images depicted on them are an intriguing subject all of their own. The Romans started it all with a welcoming sign showing a bunch of vine leaves to denote a *taberna*. As with any other commercial enterprise, pubs used signs or symbols to signify the nature of the business going on within – the barber's pole and the pawnbroker's balls still survive to this day. The reason for all this symbolism was that most people could not read until the end of the nineteenth century, so words would have been quite useless. A sign, however, spoke volumes. From 1393 it was the law for innkeepers to display a sign. Pub owners accordingly invented names and signs to differentiate their pub from the one up the road or down the yard. The sign set it apart from other inns and taverns in the locality and might also advertise what might be found inside (e.g. cold meats or board games as well as ale), or indeed the political leanings of the landlord. Coats of arms reflect the custom adopted by noblemen where they displayed their banners outside the inn to show that they might be found within. York's imposing gallows sign at Ye Olde Starre Inne, spanning Stonegate, is a very rare surviving example of these literally unmissable pub indicators.

Royal Oak was a supporter of Charles II (he hid in one at Boscobel after the Battle of Worcester in 1651 before restoring the monarchy in 1660), Punch Bowl indicated a Whig, and Marquis of Granby reflected the philanthropy showed to veterans of said marquis. Chequers denoted board games while The Board proclaimed that cold meats were on offer inside – the board being what the meats were served on, hence 'board and lodge'.

In 1553 the number of pubs was restricted by law: London was allowed forty, York a mere eight and Hull a miserable three. Legislation so universally, yet happily, ignored and unenforced would be hard to find: in 1623 there were still 13,000 licensed premises in England.

In her 1698 *Through England On a Side Saddle in the Time of William and Mary*, the enterprising and fearless Celia Fiennes called in at Leeds on her trip round the kingdom and gives us a fascinating insight on the price and strength of beer here, agonising as to whether her bar meals should be on the house or not:

> Leeds is a Large town…their ale is very strong, but for paying this Groat for yo^ur^ ale you may have a slice of meate Either hott or Cold according to the tyme of day you Call, or Else butter and Cheese Gratis into the bargaine; this was a Generall Custom in most parts of Yorkshire but now they have almost Changed it, and tho' they still retaine the great price for the ale, yet Make strangers pay for their meate, and at some places at great rates, notwithstanding how Cheape they have all their provision. There is still this Custome on a Market day at Leeds, the sign of ye bush just by the Bridge, any body y^t^ will goe and Call for one tanchard of ale and a pinte of wine and pay for these only shall be set to a table to Eate wth 2 or 3 dishes of good meate and a dish of sweetmeates after. Had I known this and ye Day wch was their Market I would have Come then but I happened to Come a day after ye market, however I did only pay for 3 tankards of ale and w^t^ I Eate, and my servants was gratis.

A few years later Daniel Defoe, in his *A Tour Through the Whole Island of Great Britain*, agrees, although he is not so obsessed with the bar meals. He shows how inns and beer played an integral role in the lucrative wool and textile industry in Leeds:

> Formerly the cloth market was kept in neither part of the town, but on the very bridge it self; and therefore the refreshment given the clothiers by the inn-keepers, of which I shall speak presently is called the Brigg-shot to this day… The clothiers come early in the morning with their cloth; and as few clothiers bring more than one piece, the market being so frequent, they go into the inns and publick-houses with it, and there set it down… by half an hour after eight a clock the market bell rings again; immediately the buyers disappear, the cloth is all sold, or if here and there a piece

A nineteenth-century beerhouse.

> happens not to be bought, 'tis carried back into the inn, and, in a quarter of an hour, there is not a piece of cloth to be seen in the market.

Incidentally, Defoe wrote much of his *Robinson Crusoe* in the Rose & Crown in Halifax's Back Lane, according to his Leeds publisher, Edward Baines. The full, somewhat prolix title of the book is *The Life and Strange Surprising Adventures of Robinson Crusoe, of York, Mariner, Written by Himself.*

Pubs, then, were not always just pubs. Many doubled up as coroners' and magistrates' courts, as markets, morgues and as smugglers' dens. Others were also blacksmith's, cobblers or carpenters – often the landlord's day job. The Denmark Arms in Scarborough was also a grocers until its closure. Appropriately enough The White Boar in Huddersfield was also a butchers. Fiddling the customer has always happened: in 1734 the landlord here, John Walker, was fined for giving short measures. The Beaumont Arms at Kirkheaton, near Huddersfield, doubled as an undertakers. The Three Nuns at Mirfield was where the nuns brewed their own ale. The Cricket Inn in Sheffield's Hyde Park had its own cricket pitch from 1826, as had The Strafford Arms at Stainborough nearby. The Victoria Park Hotel in Sheffield had a bowling green and 'an American bowling alley' in the mid-1800s. The Crooked Billet at Ryhill, near Hedon, housed a slaughterhouse. Best of all, though, was The Humber Tavern in Paull, east of Hull; here in 1836

Trinity House decided that 'lights be exhibited in the windows of a public house at Paull as a temporary expedient until the erection of permanent lights'.

As noted, Wellington's Beerhouse Act of 1830 saw licensed premises double in ten years, with 25,000 new licences issued within three months of the legislation. It also galvanised the rise of the common brewery, brewing beer and selling it to other outlets rather than brewing for oneself. In 1823 Hull had 274 inns serving a population of 44,924, making one pub per 164 people. York was even better provisioned with 194 inns for 22,529 inhabitants, one for every 116 residents. Take children out of the equation and the figures are even more astonishing. Tadcaster takes the biscuit in 1837 with twenty-four inns and taverns and eleven beerhouses – thirty-five places to drink for a population of 2,400 providing one pub for every seventy people, more than twice the national average at the time. At its peak Sheffield in 1863 had 560 inns and hotels with 682 beerhouses and over 600 off-licences. Beerhouses naturally proliferated here around the steel mills and heavy engineering factories. A common sight was boys wielding broomsticks with cans suspended full of beer for the thirsty workers.

2

The Pubs

Above and opposite page: Four famous Leeds pubs.

SHIP
Quality Food

THE
CHEMIC
TAVERN

NICHOLSON'S
FREEHOUSE
SCARBROUGH
HOTEL

1. The Adelphi, Corner of Hunslet Road and Dock Street

The Grade II listed Adelphi opened its doors in 1897. 120 or so years later its small, intimate rooms with their own individual character and original fireplaces continue to delight. The four individually decorated high-ceilinged rooms can still boast lacquered Victorian carved wood, polished brass, arched and pillared doorways and etched glass.

Tetley's launched its 'Heritage Inns' scheme 1978, designed to spotlight pubs in their estate with special architectural and historic interest. They began with three pubs: The Bingley Arms in Bardsey, The Adelphi, and The Garden Gate in Hunslet.

> Inside is a cornucopia of colourful tiles and carved mahogany, etched glass and polished brass. Polished walnut, too, gleams across the floor of one of four downstairs rooms as well as the imposing function room upstairs. It's accessed via a broad and lavishly tiled staircase rising majestically from a passageway sporting a bar with a row of hand-pumps.
>
> The products of Joshua Tetley and Son would have gushed from each of them at one time. Tetley workers gathered at the Adelphi every evening to continue sampling the fruits of their labours with the draymen who humped 36-gallon barrels of the stuff down cellar steps. They were renowned for their prodigious consumption, as indeed were the dray horses that regularly found their way home to their stables with some 14 pints under their bridles. The last horse was put out to grass at the turn of the [twenty-first] century and the brewery closed in 2011.
>
> Chris Arnot, *The Telegraph*, 28 October 2014

Nos 3–5 Hunslet Road, Leeds, LS10 1JQ
0113 2456377
www.theadelphileeds.co.uk
theadelphi@live.co.uk

The Adelphi.

2. The Angel Inn, Angel Inn Yard, Briggate

The Angel Inn is situated in the Angel Yard between Lands Lane and Briggate. There has been a pub here since the Middle Ages but this inn dates from the late eighteenth century. It closed in 1903 and was then used as a business premises until converted back to a pub and reopened by Sam Smith's in 2000. The pub is 'the oldest purpose-built inn surviving in yards off Briggate'.

The Angel Inn was at one time run by the Ledgard family before they moved to the Nelson at Armley. The landlord's son, Samuel, was one of the pioneering bus operators in Leeds. The Samuel Ledgard Society preserves the memory of this famous Leeds entrepreneur.

A blue plaque on the wall outside commemorates Joseph Aspdin (1778–1855), inventor of Portland cement, who lived in the yard (then known as Slip Inn Yard), and sold his cement from there.

Angel Inn Yard, Leeds, LS1 6LN
0113 245 1428

Above right and left: The Angel inside and out.

3. The Beech, Wortley

What Pub describes it best:

> Reopened on 27th November 2015 after being closed for several years ... built in 1931 for Melbourne Brewery, much external signage and livery, including windows, of the brewery remains. A very high percentage of original internal fixtures and fittings have been retained. The large front room (Vaults) has a tiled floor, two fires and brown fixed seating against the front and side walls either side of the entrance. The dark brown bar is against the far wall complete with glass shelf suspended from the high ceiling.

There has been a public house here since the 1850s. It was approved as a Grade II listed building because of its art deco styling and distinctive cladding.

Melbourne Brewery was in Plum Street, Leeds, and registered in December 1889 as the Leeds & Wakefield Breweries Ltd to amalgamate Kirk, Matthews, Melbourne Brewery and Carter & Sons, Victoria Brewery, Wakefield. The name changed to Melbourne Brewery (Leeds) Ltd in December 1957. Acquired by Tetley in 1960, brewing ended in 1961. Melbourne had an estate of 245 public houses.

The Barchester Ales Brewery was at the other end of Tong Road. The Cemetery Hotel was at No. 67 with The Crown at No. 2 and a New Inn at No. 336.

No. 8 Tong Road, Wortley, Leeds, LS12 1HX
0113 263 8659

The mosaic celebrating Melbourne Ales.

Belgrave Vegan Feast, 2019.

4. Belgrave Music Hall and Canteen

Belgrave Music Hall and Canteen first opened its doors in 1934 as Leeds Children's Palace, a three-storey recreation hall and nursery school built to provide childcare for the working families of Leeds. After many years of neglect, the building was restored to its former glory and reopened as Belgrave Music Hall and Canteen in 2013.

No. 1a Cross Belgrave St, Leeds, LS2 8JP
0113 234 6160
www.belgravemusichall.com

5. The Black Prince, Boar Lane

The Black Prince opened for business in 1903 and reflects the fine statue that dominates City Square. The Black Prince (1330–76, eldest son of Edward III) has nothing much to do with Leeds. He was a gift to the city to celebrate Leeds' new status as a city from Colonel Thomas Walter Harding, Lord Mayor of Leeds between 1898 and 18999. The prince was just someone Harding admired, symbolising as he did the virtues of liberty and chivalry. Harding had no regrets regarding his choice, maintaining that the Black Prince was 'the hero of Crecy and Poitiers, the flower of English chivalry, the upholder of the liberties of the English people, would remain an emblem of manly and unselfish virtues.' A nymph stands in front of the prince.

The bronze sculpture was so big that it had to be cast in Belgium, as there was no foundry in Britain large enough. It was towed to Leeds via Hull by barge.

No. 40 Boar Lane, Leeds, West Yorkshire, LS1 5DA
0113 245 8063
www.theblackprinceleeds.co.uk

The Black Prince.

6. The Cardigan Arms, Kirkstall Road, Burley

Kirkstall Brewery has restored this pub back to its former glory. The 1893 Grade II listed Victorian pub exudes character, with its circular bar and snug rooms (one of which was ladies only) and sensitively refurbished fine woodwork, etched glass and ornamented ceilings. The moulded segmental pediment bears a coat of arms and motto: 'EN GOAGE AFFIE', 'Engage Affie'. Affie was Alfred (Alfred Ernest Albert, 1844–1900), who reigned as Duke of Saxe-Coburg and Gotha from 1893 to 1900. He was the second son and fourth child of Queen Victoria and Prince Albert of Saxe-Coburg and Gotha.

Here is Historic England's description of the pub's interior:

'Large central foyer with glazed double doors, tiled walls, possibly original embossed wallpaper, glazed partitions with carved Classical details, open staircase; 4 rooms open off, small rear room, all with original woodwork and glass decoration, etched and brilliant-cut glass, ornate wood and tile fireplaces; first-floor function room, "Harmonic Room" on etched glass door'.

The pub is named after James Brudenell, 7th Earl of Cardigan, which explains the painting of the charge of the Light Brigade in the front room – Cardigan was the man who led the disastrous charge against the Russians in 1854 in the Battle of Balaclava during the Crimean War.

The derelict former Cardigan Arms Brewery and stables languish in the backyard of the pub.

In 1906 the Cardigan Arms was selling twenty hogsheads a week (one hogshead is 54 gallons or 432 pints). That's 8,640 pints a week.

No. 364 Kirkstall Road, Leeds, West Yorkshire, LS4 2HQ
0113 226 3154
www.cardiganarms.co.uk
info@cardiganarms.co.uk

The Cardigan Arms with its splendid chandelier.

7. The Chemic Tavern, Johnston Street

The early nineteenth-century, delightfully named Chemic Tavern is by the junction with Woodhouse and Beulah Street. The pub got its name from nearby Johnston's Chemical Works, just over the road, which produced Vitriol – sulphuric acid – up until the 1890s and would have been used by the tanneries and dyeworks of the Meanwood Valley. The factory was demolished in the 1890s, but 'the pub has endured as a popular community hub, welcoming creatives, musicians and local residents for decades.'

> All of human life can be glimpsed here. Where else could you stumble upon a chap entertaining drinkers with his home-made clarinet, or a Breton music group, or a lipsync contest, which is essentially karaoke but without the singing?... If you fancy a game of Scrabble, or somewhere to sit with a book, or watch a band, or just enjoy a great beer, the Chemic really has the formula.
>
> *Yorkshire Evening Post,* 16 April 2015

Entertainment comes thick and fast, and is nothing if not truly eclectic. Here is the programme for the first week of June 2019: 'Quiz Night; The Muzikantes European Jam Session; The Chemic Singers; Open Ukelele Session; Open Irish Session; French Breton; Shackleford, Skiv and Chrissy Orlando; Hot Tin Roof Comedy Final; Lazy Sunday 'Craft'ernoon'. And don't forget the Balkan disco, and the lip sync contest, karaoke without the singing.

Leeds, indeed, is a good example of a city that celebrates local industry and trades through its pub names. Apart from the Chemic you can, or more often could, raise an arm and a glass in the

Inside the Chemic Tavern.

The big bar bell. (Courtesy of the Chemic Tavern)

Blacksmiths Arms, Bricklayers Arms, Brassmoulders Arms, Butchers Arms (Batley), Carpenters Arms, Carriers Arms in Morley, Farmers Arms, Fellmongers Arms, Ostlers Arms, Plasterers Arms and Skinners Arms. Work is clearly thirsty work.

Johnston Street, Woodhouse, Leeds, LS6 2NG
0113 245 7670
www.chemictavern.co.uk
hello@chemictavern.co.uk

8. The Clothiers Arms, Yeadon

More industrial thirst-slaking here. Yeadon is a former mill town specialising in the production of woollen cloth.

No. 56 High Street, Yeadon, Leeds, LS19 7PP
0113 238 6970

The Clothiers Arms.

9. The Cross Keys, Water Lane

This venerable old pub was built in 1802 as another watering hole to slake the prodigious thirsts of workers from nearby industry – in this case local foundry workers. Industrial espionage was rife here when, soon after opening, industrial engineer and inventor of the modern steam engine James Watt, of Birmingham's Boulton and Watt, hired a room in the pub from which he allegedly spent three months spying on local engineer and rival Matthew Murray, as well as filching trade secrets from Murray's workers who were innocently drinking in the pub.

In the 1980s The Cross Keys closed and was left to dilapidate. It was used by a local garage to store tyres, but help came when an extensive refit reanimated this social and historical landmark from the heyday of Leeds' industrial past. James Watt is on hand to greet you as you make your way up the beautiful fairylight-lit spiral staircase.

Matthew Murray presented Boulton and Watt with a problem, for it was he who designed and built the first steam locomotive (the twin cylinder *Salamanca* in 1812), revolutionised flax spinning machinery at Marshall's Mill in Holbeck and opened his own Round Foundry (a huge three-storeyed circular building) nearby. The duplicitous Watt deployed engineers from his Midlands works to spy on Murray's plant (although in the event it seems that a naïve Murray showed and explained everything to his curious visitors anyway). He challenged Murray's patents to confound him with legalese and red tape, patents which included flax-spinning machines of his own design (1790), a design for 'Instruments and Machines for Spinning Fibrous Materials' (1793), a carding engine and a spinning machine that introduced the new technique of 'wet spinning' flax, which revolutionised the flax trade. Finally, James Watt Jr bought land around Murray's Round Foundry to prevent the business from expanding.

No. 107 Water Lane, Leeds, LS11 5WD
0113 243 3711
www.the-crosskeys.com
info@the-crosskeys.com

The Collier aquatint by Robert Havell after George Walker, published in 1814, from Costumes of Yorkshire, showing Blenkinsop's rack locomotive *Salamanca* on the Middleton Railway. The image features the earliest known representation of a steam train.

10. The Crowd of Favours, Harper Street

Just off Kirkgate and close to the market, a £100,000 refurbishment by owners Cameron's of Hartlepool has made this a smart place to go, despite the elephant in the room.

Harper Street, Leeds, West Yorkshire, LS2 7EA
0113 246 9405
www crowdoffavours.co.uk
info@crowdoffavours.co.uk

The elephant in the room.

Not much of a crowd here.

11. The Drysalters, Elland Road

The name comes from the occupation of its first licensee in 1834 – one Joseph Lee, who was listed as a 'drysalter, oil dealer, preparer of peachwood, camwood, cotton manufacturer and victualer of the Drysalters Arms'.

A football pub on match days that is especially welcoming to away supporters – honest.

Elland Road, Leeds, LS11 8AX
0113 270 0229
www.drysaltersnew.co.uk

12. The Duck & Drake, Kirkgate

Adapted from the excellent website:

> History is important at The Duck & Drake - history of Leeds, of Beer, of pubs, even the history of live music – some of which is depicted on a massive mural across the back wall of the bar. Today the Duck & Drake still has examples of its' Victorian beginnings. With a typically Victorian façade, the marble doorway jambs are also a fine example of the era. There are a number of original light fittings and the floorboards in both bars have survived 200 years of trade ... The pub was bought by Jim Wright who created the TFC alehouses [named after] The Fighting Cock (hence TFC) in Bradford... The pub has existed under several different names including The Horse & Groom and the The Brougham's Arms ... It wasn't until 1985 that the name changed to The Duck & Drake. Though you would be forgiven for thinking the name refers to waterfowl, it doesn't. It actually alludes to the long-gone pastime of skimming stones on water called 'ducks & drakes'.

No. 43 Kirkgate, Leeds, LS2 7DR
0113 245 5432
www.ducknddrake.co.uk

The Duck & Drake with rock heroes mural.

13. The Duncan, Duncan Street

Some say that it's named after Leeds United legend Duncan McKenzie, but the street name in which the pub stands may just have something to do with it. Anyway, McKenzie made sixty-six appearances for Leeds between 1974 and 1976, hitting the back of the net twenty-seven times.

Duncan Street was once Fleet Street but this was changed after the Napoleonic Wars, when Admiral Adam Duncan (1731–1804) scored a glorious victory over the Dutch fleet at the Battle of Camperdown (north of Haarlem) in 1797, one of the most significant actions in Royal Navy history. Fleet Street was rebadged in his honour and the pub was the icing on the cake.

The other Duncan, in the Headrow, was, after the Whip, the second to last pub in Leeds to permit women through the door in the early 1980s.

Nos 22–26 Duncan Street, Leeds, LS1 6DL
0113 245 9916
www.twitter.com/duncanpub

14. The Fleece, Farsley

The Fleece, on Town Street in Farsley, was the second of the pubs bought by Tetley's as the brewery expanded at the end of the nineteenth century. The Fleece was acquired by Tetley's in 1890 soon after the Duke William. A blue plaque on the building's front wall says: 'This plaque was erected to commemorate the fact that the Fleece, Farsley, is the oldest original licensed Joshua Tetley public house. The pub was purchased by the company on 11 November 1890 for £2,206-15s-5d.'

No. 116 Town Street, Farsley, Pudsey, Leeds, LS28 5LF
0113 257 7683
www.thefleecefarsley.co.uk

The Old Hall Hotel, the other pub in Farsley, as run by Ann Slater.

Mr Foley's.

15. Foley's Cask Alehouse, the Headrow

Located in an imposing and very impressive edifice – Pearl Chambers – it was built of Portland stone in 1911 and was originally owned by the Pearl Assurance Company. The company was founded by Patrick James Foley, hence the name of the pub and his statue at the top of the building flanked by a pair of griffins.

Patrick James Foley (1836–1914) was born in Leeds and educated at Catholic schools in Prescot and Leeds. In 1864 he founded the Pearl Life Assurance Loan and Investment Company Ltd, renamed the Pearl Life Assurance Company in 1874, and was later president.

From an 1847 Ordnance Survey map of Leeds we can see that there were no fewer than twelve inns in the Head Row area. All of them fronted onto the Headrow, except for the Marquis of Granby Inn and the Malt Mill Inn, which were in yards to the north of the Lower Head Row. Most, if not all, of these inns were open in the seventeenth century, and some even earlier. The inns on the north-east side of the Headrow were all demolished when the street was widened in the 1920s. The Nag's Head, the Wheatsheaf, the King's Arms and the Unicorn all fronted onto the Headrow.

No. 159 the Headrow, Leeds, West Yorkshire, LS1 5RG
0113 242 9674
mrfoleyscaskalehouse@hotmail.co.uk

16. The Fox & Newt, Burley Street

At the top of Burley Road, straight opposite Park Lane College, this is probably Leeds' last remaining city centre brew-pub: 'it now plays host to Burley Street Brewhouse,' the microbrewery in the cellar of the Fox & Newt pub. The brewery was first installed by Whitbread in the 1980s.

The pub is over 150 years old and was originally a one-bedroom hotel called The Rutland. It was extended in the 1920s and then blown up in a gas explosion. When it was it reopened it was the Fox & Newt and had been expanded into a neighbouring shop.

Fox & Newt.

No. 9 Burley Street, Leeds, LS3 1LD
0113 245 4527
www.burleystreetbrewhouse.co.uk/?page_id=44

17. Friends of Ham, No. 4 New Station Street

Friends of Ham describe themselves as specialists 'in the finest charcuterie, cheese, craft beer and wine. A continental-style cafe bar'.

No. 4 New Station Street, Leeds, LS1 5DL
0113 242 0275
www.friendsofham.co.uk
trotters@friendsofham.com

Friends of Ham with explanatory drawing.

18. The Garden Gate, Hunslet

From the website:

> the pub also offers a unique chance to experience a wonderful slice of Leeds' history. In recognition of its historical, cultural and architectural importance the pub has just received a Grade II* Listing by English Heritage making it one of only a handful of pubs in the country to hold this honour... saved from closure by Leeds Brewery...[The monthly] Hunslet Hawks Heritage meeting [is when] former rugby players, people interested in Hunslet [come together].

The players' showers and communal bath are still there in the cellars, memorials to the glorious past. The pub building you see today dates from 1903, but there are records relating to the site dating from 1823, when Thomas Walton of Hunslet, a gardener, purchased a plot of land measuring 344 yards at 3*s* 3*d* per yard for a total of £55 18*s*.

In his will of 18 April 1829, Thomas Walton bequeathed his Hunslet estate to Merwyn Richards of Leeds, captain and adjutant of the first York Militia, and William Heaton the Younger of Hunslet, a maltster, with the proviso that his wife Sarah was allowed to occupy or receive rental and profits from this real estate during her lifetime.

Around 1833 we get the first mention of an inn, with Sarah being described as an innkeeper 'which occupation she carries out in Hunslet in and upon a certain dwelling house and premises late of the estate of the said Thomas Walton'.

Sarah died in 1841, and the estate was purchased by Henry Williamson, an innkeeper, in 1849, with the pub now referred to as The Garden Gate, derived from the nearby market gardens that were a source of substantial local income at the time. In 1881 Edward Wilson

The Garden Gate with brewery shires.

bought the freehold, and in 1903 built the building that we see today. It is typical of a small late Victorian, early Edwardian pub with its separate rooms and central corridor. It boasts 'a decorative treatment which rivals that of much larger city centre "gin palaces" of the period' and 'a wealth of internal riches that include lavish tilling, faience and etched glass with art nouveau motifs, mosaic floors, moulded plasterwork and ornate mahogany fitments.'

Then there is this from the *Yorkshire Evening Post*, 25 June 2015:

> It is a ceramic palace, from the ornate brown and cream tiled exterior, to the greens of the pub's long central corridor which divides little snugs, nooks and crannies from the two main drinking areas which are either side of a central bar. The corridor is itself a gem, tiled from floor to ceiling, save for polished mahogany panels and panes of etched and decorated glass. The floor is an ornate tiled mosaic; a tiled archway arcs over the corridor. Wood, mirrors and glass predominate in each room.

After Wilson's death in 1910 the pub was leased to the Bradford brewer William Whittaker & Co. Ltd, thus starting a period of brewery ownership that remained almost uninterrupted until the present day. In 1922 Ind Coope first leased and then bought the building, and Tetley took over in 1964.

In 1978 it was one of three of the houses in Tetley's inaugural 'Heritage Inns' scheme, along with the Bingley Arms in Bardsey and the Adelphi.

In 2010 it was purchased by Leeds Brewery, saving it from closure. At the same time English Heritage upgraded the pub's listed status to Grade II*; their reasons included 'the curved ceramic bar counter, which is one of only 14 ceramic bar counters surviving nationally,' noting 'the level of intactness throughout is unusually high, and nationally very rare.'

'This one of the finest examples of an untouched Victorian pub in the city. It has an original faience facade, intricate [Burmantofts] tiling, etched windows and mahogany screens, as well as a curving ceramic bar top. This is a beautiful place for a pint.'

'Suzanne', in a tweet from 2014, tells the story of how this jewel of a pub was saved from the barbarians at the council, and from Tetleys:

The Garden Gate, in Hunslet, was my grandparents' pub. They owned it from the mid 50's to the early 70's. They, along with students at Leak Street Flats, saved the pub from demolition. I remember it all like it was yesterday. One of the leading students would become very famous, you may know his name – Mark Knopfler from Dire Straits! I've amassed hundreds of photographs of the pub during these years and plan to publish a book, along with the factual events that lead up to the pub being saved FROM the council AND Tetley's demands that it be demolished! It's not quite the fairy story they have managed to paint over the years. For one, Tetley's held my grandfather hostage, denying/postponing beer deliveries while he battled them!

No. 3 Whitfield Place, Hunslet, Leeds, LS10 2QB
0113 3451234
www.gardengateleeds.co.uk/history.php
info@gardengateleeds.co.uk

19. The General Eliott, Vicar Lane

George Augustus Eliott, 1st Baron Heathfield, PC, KB (b. 1717) was a British Army officer who first made his mark during the Seven Years' War, but is most notable for his command and successful defence of the Gibraltar garrison during the Great Siege of Gibraltar (between 1779 and 1783) during the American War of Independence.

General Eliott.

Nos 31–33 Vicar Lane, Leeds, LS1 6DS
0113 244 2663

20. The Green Dragon, also The Guildford, Guildford Street

The present building is Victorian/Edwardian, but *Jackson's Guide* of 1889 tells us that the inn has a much earlier origin: 'An old grey public house fronting the street at Merryboys Hill, adjoining the road to Bradford, the resort of clothiers, was called the Duncan Inn before it became the Green Dragon.' An old print confirms this description. The pub was rebuilt at the end of the nineteenth century as a three-storey building, of stone and brick, with arched windows and elaborate carving on the front. The sandstone figures at either end are Atlantes, usually depicted naked, but in this case partly clothed in deference to the good burghers of Leeds.

It was situated in Butts Court at Merry Boys Hill, and for many years this name was remembered in the new Guildford pub, the Merry Boys Bar.

The pub changed hands in 1920–21, and its name from the Green Dragon to Hotel Guildford (that part of the Head Row was actually Guildford Street at that time). The inn was described in the 1919 sale brochure as an 'old established fully licensed hotel' with among other things 'an imposing billiard room with accommodation for four tables' on the ground floor. There was a dining room, two smoke rooms, a private sitting room, committee room, clubroom, and two bedrooms on the first floor with a further four bedrooms on the second floor.

In 1975 it was no longer a residential hotel, and in 1984, Tetley's, the owners, planned to demolish it. The plans were described by one outraged councillor as 'an act of vandalism'. The vandalistic proposal was refused. An alternative proposal was to retain the pub frontage and rebuild the pub further down the Headrow. This was presumably refused also, because in 1985, Tetley's announced a £1 million redevelopment scheme, to make extensive internal improvements and alterations to the exterior. Work began in 1986, and the Guildford was once again open to the public by the end of 1987. The pub changed again and was the city's first non-smoking bar, aptly named Oxygen. In 1988 the building won the second Leeds Award for Architecture for an altered building. Just shows, doesn't it: demolish in haste, repent at length…

21. The Griffin, Boar Lane

The 1872 Grade II listed Griffin on Boar Lane was previously known as Bar Censsa and before that The Griffin Hotel, a coaching inn from at least the seventeenth century. It was rebuilt as a railway hotel for the Leeds New station, which opened in 1869 and was owned by the joint London & North West Railway and North East Railway. One of the top hotels in Leeds, it nevertheless closed in 1999. The Gothic Revival building boasted a unique Potts clock at the corner of the building and the hours were ingeniously replaced by the words 'Griffin Hotel'.

The Griffin.

Inside the Griffin.

Another pub with an interesting clock is The New Inn in Barwick-in-Elmet, which, instead of numbers on the dial, bears the sonorous words 'No Tick'.

For many, though, the Griffin will be cherished as the place where Leeds United was born, hosting the meeting that led to the formation of the club. Leeds United's predecessors, Leeds City, was elected to league membership in 1905 but Leeds City were forcibly disbanded and forced to sell off all their players by the Football League in 1919 because of allegations of illegal payments to players during the First World War. In 1919, Leeds United was formed and were invited to join the Midland League, taking the place vacated by Leeds City Reserves. Following the dissolving of Leeds City, Yorkshire Amateurs bought their stadium, Elland Road. Yorkshire Amateurs offered to make way for the new team, and on 31 May 1920, Leeds United were elected to the Football League. The rest is history.

No. 31 Boar Lane, Leeds, West Yorkshire, LS1 5DF
0113 245 2803

The Grove Inn.

22. The Grove, Back Row, Holbeck

Standing defiantly as it does in the shadow of the twenty-first-century Bridgewater Place skyscraper, the Grove is happy to let the future pass it by, stuck firmly as it is in the nineteenth century. The place is rightly famous for its live music, its annual festival and its folk nights – long may they continue. The folk club has convened every Friday since 1962, reputedly the oldest folk club in the world, while there is a live band playing every Thursday, Saturday and Sunday night.

Back Row, Leeds, LS11 5PL
0113 244 2085
www.thegroveleeds.co.uk
thegroveleeds@gmail.com

23. The Head of Steam, Mill Hill

The pub, indeed the chain, is owned by Cameron's of Hartlepool, who for sixty years had ruby-red Strongarm as the staple of their trade. Now a smaller craft brewing plant allows them to try some low-volume alternatives and seasonal brews. HoS customers have been guinea pig samplers for several of them.

No. 12 Mill Hill, Leeds, LS1 5DQ
01132 436618
www.theheadofsteam.co.uk
leeds@theheadofsteam.co.uk

The Horse & Trumpet.

24. The Horse & Trumpet, The Headrow

The first record comes in 1788 but the present pub dates from 1825. It has long been associated with the Yorkshire Hussars Cavalry Regiment (originally the 1794 Yorkshire West Riding Yeomanry). Hence all the cavalry paraphernalia on the façade. The grey above the front portico is that of a cavalry hunter (according to the plaque); a troop comprised 50 or so officers and men, including two trumpeters.

Nos 51–53 the Headrow, Leeds, LS1 6LR
0113 243 0338
horseandtrumpet.leeds@stonegatepubs.com

25. The Kirkstall Bridge

Run by the Kirkstall Brewery and recently named in the top ten riverside pubs nationwide by the Canal and River Trust. Whatpub.com says: 'This multiple CAMRA pub of the year winner is a living museum of breweriana. Spread over two floors with an extensive riverside beer garden ... Frequent events include the annual Kirkstapalooza music and beer festival and hugely popular bonfire night.' Lauren James in *Time Out* adds:

> The décor is simple and traditional, apart from the many reclaimed beer-related paintings, photographs and mirrors that festoon the walls...and there's a beer garden overlooking the water making outdoor drinking idyllic in summer (5 November 2014).

Leeds pub garden floods but men go for pints anyway…

After the outside of their pub flooded in Leeds, there was only one thing to do for John Kelly and Steve Holt: '"The water came in pretty quickly and pretty heavily and once we realised, Steve (the pub's owner) drove off to get some sandbags", the manager of the Kirkstall Bridge Inn tells [BBC's] *Newsbeat* 16.11.15 … "I stood and shouted at the water but it didn't seem to do much. The water came to within a couple of feet of the Kirkstall Bridge Inn's back door. It was remarkably cold. The first 15 minutes were a little bit uncomfortable but once we settled down it was surprisingly therapeutic, to sit not just by the river but in the river" … "A crowd gathered and eventually we got shouted out by Steve's missus and we had to get out like naughty little boys".'

Bridge Road, Kirkstall, Leeds, LS5 3BW
0113 278 4044
www.kirkstallbridge.co.uk
info@kirkstallbridge.co.uk

26. The Lamb & Flag, Church Row

A nineteenth-century Leeds Brewery tavern in the shadow of Leeds Minster. It gets its name from the crest of the Merchant Taylors' Company, which is very fitting in a tailoring city like Leeds.

The company started as an association of working tailors, known as the Fraternity of St John the Baptist. This was both for trade regulation and insurance, for a good funeral and for prayers for one's soul in Purgatory after death. Later the company was known as the Company of Tailors and Linen-Armourers, linen armour being the padded clothes worn under metal armour.

The company went from strength to strength and many prominent people were admitted to the Fraternity, such as Henry V. By the late fifteenth century the senior membership contained an increasing number of wealthy merchants who traded within England and also overseas. The company became the Company of Merchant Taylors by a royal charter of 1503. A few years later it also became one of the 'Great Twelve' livery companies, the senior companies in the city from which all Lord Mayors were chosen.

No. 1 Church Row, Leeds, West Yorkshire, LS2 7HD
0113 243 1255
info@lambandflagleeds.co.uk

The Lamb & Flag.

27. Leeds Postal Service, Wellington Street

Open in West Point on Wellington Street, Leeds Postal Service was formerly known as Royal Mail House. West Point was originally built in 1975 and renovated in 2005 as a huge redevelopment of the old Royal Mail building site, which is home to several venues including Toast Bar, Primo Lounge and Leeds Postal Services sister venue, Lazy Lounge.

'Its main "Sorting Office" space features giant factory striplights, scaffolding railings, discarded beer barrels, high steel tables and simple wooden stools. A giant post office clock hangs above the bar, a meandering trail of ivy is a small concession to nature, while beer cans have been repurposed into a colourful art installation'. *Yorkshire Evening Post*, 11 October 2018

West Point, Wellington Street, Leeds, LS1 4JY
0113 430 0232
www.leedspostalservice.co.uk

28. The Midnight Bell, Holbeck

Leeds Brewery's flagship pub, 'With the perfect mixture of traditional and contemporary features our oak beams and ancient brickwork sit alongside a concrete bar and high wide windows.'

The website tells us that

> Sam Moss and Michael Brothwell met at university and after graduating, decided to open their own brewery. In June 2007 Leeds Brewery opened its doors as the only independent brewery in the city… Today the brewery produces over 70,000 pints a week…In 2008 Leeds Brewery opened its first pub, The Midnight Bell. Since then the brewery has opened another five sites. All are distinctly different, ranging from red bricks fired at the start of the industrial revolution at The Midnight Bell, to original etched and bevelled glass work at The Garden Gate, to 13th century timber frames at The Duke of York.

No. 101 Water Lane, Leeds, LS11 5QN
0113 244 5044
www.midnightbell.co.uk
info@midnightbell.co.uk

The Moot Hall Arms.

29. The Moot Hall Arms

This pub's former names include the Waiting Rooms, Baht'ap and Prince of Wales.

No. 11 Mill Hill, Leeds, LS1 5DQ
0113 244 2433
www.moothallarms-leeds.craftunionpubs.com

30. The Morley Dashers, Morley

The Morley Dashers is so named after the piece workers who took finished cloth from Morley to Leeds and then dashed back for more.

No. 66 High Street, Morley, Leeds, LS27 0BY
0113 253 4945
www.morleydashers.co.uk/

31. The Nags Head, Chapel Allerton

The Nags Head opened in 1772 on the turnpike road between Leeds and Harrogate when Chapel Allerton was no more than a few farms, cottages, a quarry and some big houses. The structure is largely unchanged and a mounting stone and serving window are still there. Allegedly the original innkeepers were complicit with local footpads, smugglers and bodysnatchers and the like. 'Under the stone flags of the cellars [was] found a black door, beyond which was a deeper cellar which led out onto a tunnel. The underground passage led to a neighbouring churchyard, and at the end of the passage was a stone slab with human remains on.'

No. 20 Town Street, Leeds, LS7 4NB
0113 262 4938

32. The Nation of Shopkeepers, Cookridge Street

The phrase 'a nation of shopkeepers' (*une nation de boutiquiers*) is attributed to Napoleon as a derogatory reference to England; there is, however, no evidence that he ever uttered those words.

Nos 27–37 Cookridge Street, Leeds, LS2 3AG
0113 203 1831
www.anationofshopkeepers.com

33. The New Inn, Headingley

Opened in 1842, its bay windows still bear the etching 'Bentley's Yorkshire Breweries'. This is one of around fifteen New Inns in Leeds, making it the most popular pub name locally. A further ten or so have been and gone. This is the pub that has the famous 'no tick clock'. It started life as the New Inn, making it an old inn today, but it went through a period masquerading as an Irish pub called O'Hagans. Now it has reverted back to being the New Inn. The pub is stop three on the Otley Run.

No. 68 Otley Road, Leeds, LS6 4BA
0113 224 9131
www.greeneking-pubs.co.uk

34. The New Penny, Call Lane

Probably the oldest gay pub in Leeds and the first gay venue to open outside of London, it started out as the Hope & Anchor in 1953, obviously as a clandestine place. It is thought that it is the longest continually running gay venue in the UK. In March 1968, the Hope & Anchor was featured in an exposé in the local *Union News*, which was soon reprinted in *The People*. Inevitably, the pub was targeted and 'completely wrecked' by football fans following the Leeds United vs Glasgow Rangers match at Elland Road on 9 April 1968. It closed for a while, and after a change of ownership it reopened as The New Penny.

The famous blue plaque.

The New Penny.

The pub has featured some of the best-known drag queens including Lily Savage, Anna Glypta, Fats and Small, Sisters Slim, Amber Dextrous, Miss Orry, Ricky Glass and more beside. It is still one of the most popular venues in Leeds, attracting both gays and straights.

No. 57 Call Lane, Leeds, LS1 7BT
0113 243 8055

35. The North Bar, New Briggate

North Brewing Co. was founded in 2015 by John Gyngell and Christian Townsley, the men behind legendary Leeds beer venue North Bar, which opened in 1997. Known as 'the first craft beer bar in Britain', North Bar has apparently influenced a new wave of modern beer bars and breweries across the country, including their own.

No. 24 New Briggate, Leeds, LS1 6NU
0113 242 4540
www.northbar.com

36. Northern Monk Refectory, Marshall Street

The Old Flax Store in Marshall's Mill is a Grade II listed building in Holbeck, the heart of Leeds's industrial revolution. In 2014 Northern Monk turned this derelict mill into a brewery, tap room and events space. This building is home to their first brewery on the ground floor of the building.

John Marshall, after whom the street is named, is one of the great industrialists of Leeds. He was nothing if not architecturally flamboyant. His flax mills in Holbeck are still there on Marshall Street but his most famous and splendidly unorthodox is a full-scale replica of the ancient Egyptian temple at Edfu, which opened in 1838. The Temple of Edfu is dedicated to the falcon god Horus, built sometime in the Ptolemaic period between 237 and 57 BCE.

Marshall was one of the pioneers of workers' safety and education and did much to mitigate the dangers inherent in running and working in a textile mill. He was only too aware of the flammability of textiles and so built twenty-five fire escapes into his building; multi-storey to him spelled death trap, with carnage and mayhem a possibility on stairways so he made Temple Works single storey. Like Rowntree, Titus Salt and Cadbury he felt a social responsibility towards his workers and their families : the undercroft housed children's dormitories, shops, doctors, a church; there was a school adjacent to the mill at ground level.

The children, until aged twelve, were well looked after while their parents worked close by to bring home the bacon.

Northern Monk Refectory, Marshall's Mill, Marshall Street, Holbeck, Leeds, LS11 9YP
0113 243 6430
www.northernmonk.com
drink@northernmonk.com

37. The Old Ball, Brownberrie Lane, Horsforth

Some say it was named after balls delivered at Horsforth Cricket club next door. However, another attempt at the etymology is more interesting: in 1773 tanner Jacob Edmundson was granted a licence to serve beer on land which had belonged to the Stanhope family. A name had to be found and the family decided on the old 'bull', the bull being a family pet. However, illegible handwriting was misread as 'ball' – and 'ball' has remained ever since.
Coincidentally, the pub has enjoyed long associations with sports: Knurr and Speel an old 'catch' game is said to have been played in the field next door; cock fighting, and cricket, which is still played thereabouts, were popular. The pub was an official meeting place for tenant farmers who would congregate to pay their rent to the Stanhopes. The original building was demolished in 1969 and the present one built a short distance back from the road.

Brownberrie Lane, Horsforth, Leeds, LS18 5SB
0113 258 9139
www.theoldballleeds.co.uk

38. The Old Peacock, Elland Road

Opposite the Leeds United football ground, the pub gave the club its original nickname, not the other way round. Elland Road has been the home of Leeds United AFC since the club was founded in 1919; previously the ground was occupied by Leeds City FC and Holbeck Rugby Club. Bentley's Brewery owned it under the name of the Old Peacock Ground, after the nearby pub – hence the club's nickname, the Peacocks.

No. 251 Elland Road, Leeds, LS11 8TU
0113 271 59 62
www.theoldpeacock.co.uk/Contactus.aspx
theoldpeacock@ossett-brewery.co.uk

39. The Old Red Lion, Meadow Lane

'The attractive, curving oak-panelled bar is topped with a line of the distinctive box-shaped illuminated fonts serving the whole company [Sam Smith's] range. Art deco lanterns hang beside rows of gleaming pint glasses, just above eye level.'

Meadow Lane, Leeds, LS1 7BT
0113 443 2833

40. The Old Unicorn, Bramley

The OS map of Bramley for 1890 shows the pub, and a difficult-to-decipher old date stone, in the outdoor seating area, shows the year '1877', which might be when the present building was erected. This pub, or an earlier of the same name, is recorded in a local directory published

The Old Unicorn.

in 1822, possibly dating from the eighteenth century. Stone-built, it is set on a small hill above Bramley Town Street.

No. 165 Town Street, Bramley, LS13 3NA
0113 255 5001

41. The Pack Horse, Pack Horse Yard, off Briggate

The Templar cross can be seen at the front of this ancient pub in Pack Horse Yard, off Briggate. The cross tells us that it was originally part of the Manor of Whitkirk, which was owned by the Order of St John of Jerusalem, successors to the Knights Templar. The Harrison Arms in Harrison Street and the Old George Commercial Hotel also bear a Templar cross.

The Pack Horse opened in 1615, although there may have been a drinking house on the site in the 1500s, and some say this goes back to the 1130s. In 1615 it was the (K)Nag's Head and then the Slip Inn from 1770. It entertained Royalists during the English Civil War, it was home to a dancing school from 1750 and it's been a theatre bar looking after actors and audiences from the nearby City Varieties. There is a legend that in 1643, when Leeds was retaken from the Royalists by Sir Thomas Fairfax, the riotous victors were given a month's free entertainment at the Pack Horse in exchange for foregoing the usual rape and pillage. No doubt the one thing soon led to the other anyway.

In 1987 the Pack Horse narrowly escaped being demolished due to appeals from the Victorian Society; however, the pub was later knocked down and rebuilt on the site of the old cellars, with the Templar cross.

In 1750, Mr. Joseph Baker of London opened a posh dancing academy in one of the rooms, 'where ladies and gentlemen may depend upon being instructed in the best manner'. It also was involved in one of the earliest wireless developments in Leeds. In 1910, by arrangement with the Post Office, the Queen's Theatre, City Varieties, Pack Horse and Scarborough Taps were all wired to each other's bars. There were six pairs of headphones in each bar, enabling customers to hear performers across the city.

Pack Horse Yard, Briggate, Leeds, West Yorkshire, LS1 6AT
0113 2341311
www.thepackhorseleeds.co.uk

Above left: The Pack Horse.

Above right: An early photo clearly showing the cross in its original position.

42. The Packhorse, Woodhouse Lane

Across the road from Leeds University's engineering buildings, the Packhorse opened in 1871 and still displays some of the design features popular in pubs of that time.

'The central corridor has doors to left and right leading into compact little snugs, some with the original fitted seating around the walls, and other genuine Victorian artefacts like tiled fireplaces, attractively-fashioned armrests and bell-pushes to summon table service'. *Yorkshire Evening Post*, 17 March 2011

No. 208 Woodhouse Lane, Leeds LS2 9DX
0113 245 3980

43. The Palace, Kirkgate

The building dates back to 1741 when it was constructed as a home for a timber merchant. The Palace became a pub in 1841, assuming the name of the brewery from which it bought its beer. Henry Teall was the first landlord. He was also a boat maker, which explains the long passage which leads from the old cellars down to the canal. Inside, each room wraps around a huge curved bar.

From 1874, it was owned by the Castelow family, who brewed their own beer and all lie buried in St Peter's graveyard next door. It was bought by Melbourne Breweries in 1926, then Tetley's in the 1960s. It is now owned by Mitchell and Butler. The Palace is haunted by the ghost of Michael Hill, a Leeds actor, singer, poet and entertainer, who dropped dead there in 1948. A benefit concert was later held in the pub for his widow and family.

Kirkgate, Leeds, LS2 7DJ
0113 244 5882
www.thepalaceleeds.co.uk

44. The Podger, Ninelands Lane, Garforth

This name comes from a small engineering firm called Archibald's, which closed in the 1950s when the land was bought by Tetley's to create a new pub for Garforth. The brewery asked Mr Archibald to suggest a name. He came up with 'The Podger' after a tool his firm invented. The spanner on the inn sign remembers the pub's industrial heritage.

Ninelands Lane, Garforth, Leeds, LS25 1NT
0113 286 4796
www.thepodgerleeds.co.uk
bun212813@mbplc.com

45. The Preston, Roundhay Road

The name Preston is named after Thomas Preston, a Chapel Allerton grocer who built the building in 1898. When he died in 1902, his son, Thomas Issott Preston, a pharmacist, occupied the premises for over thirty years in his chemist's shop. The mosaic floor at the door's threshold, emblazoned with the name 'Preston', dates from this period. Indeed, the *Yorkshire Evening Post* describes how it reuses 'the shapely carved woodwork of the shopfront and the amber and black floor tiles where customers will once have waited for the dispenser to work his alchemy with mortar and pestle' (2 September 2013). It is part of the North Bar empire.

No. 468 Roundhay Road, Oakwood, Leeds, LS8 2HU
0113 249 4709
www.northbar.com/preston

46. The Regent, Kirkgate

The Regent is found just over the road from Leeds Markets. Most pubs called 'The Regent' refer to the Prince Regent, the future George IV. At one time there were three of them in Leeds alone. The others are the unmistakably Irish pub just outside the city centre which was also known as Maguire's until its demolition some years ago and one in Chapel Allerton.

No. 109 Kirkgate, Leeds, LS1 6DP
01132 435 476

47. The Reliance, North Street

> The Reliance is an outfit with both heart and brain engaged, exactly the sort of place I hope to find on my travels. It calls itself "an informal pub" and you can have just a pint and a first-class fish-finger sarnie, but that would be to miss a real trick. The street level, with its scuffed wooden floors, soaring, curved windows (one of which announces, endearingly, "Ey up") and blackboards is a lovely place to while away an hour or so. But up a few stairs is a light-filled dining room of scrubbed simplicity, with no fancy decor to detract from its focal point, an entirely open kitchen. Here, a lanky chap carves charcuterie into paper-thin slices. And it's this that has drawn me in: they make it all in-house, everything from lomo to soppressata, butchering whole pigs from "our friends the farmers at Taste Tradition near Thirsk". In their curing room, fat sausages age gracefully, hams slowly become drier and saltier, salamis inhale the fragrances of chilli and black pepper.
>
> Marina O'Loughlin, *The Guardian*, 18 July 2014

Outside the Reliance.

> The Reliance on North Street is aptly named, for it truly is a bastion of reliability. It has been in situ for more than two decades, during which time it has cemented its reputation as one of the most capable, not to mention enjoyable and constantly inventive destinations in the city.
>
> *Yorkshire Evening Post*, 7 December 2018

Nos 76–78 North Street, Leeds, LS2 7PN
0113 295 6060
www.the-reliance.co.uk/

48. The Roundhay Fox, Princes Avenue

The Roundhay Fox emerged from two Italian restaurants, a tea shop and a wine bar known as The Stables. Roundhay Park is one of the biggest city parks in Europe, extending more than 700 acres of parkland, lakes, woodland and gardens, and just short of a million people visit each year. Only Richmond Park, Phoenix Park (Dublin) and the Silesian Culture and Recreation Park (Chorzów, Poland) are bigger.

The park has a distinguished history. William the Conqueror granted the lands on which the park stands to the Normandy knight Ilbert De Lacy for his support in the savage Harrying of the North in the winter of 1069–70. De Lacy went on to found Pontefract Castle. During the thirteenth century, the area was used as a hunting park for the De Lacys, who were then the lords of Bowland on the Yorkshire–Lancaster border. Ownership of Roundhay passed through

The Roundhay Fox.

succession to John of Gaunt and then to his son, Henry IV. In the sixteenth century Henry VIII gave the park, but not the manor, to Thomas Darcy.

Princes Avenue, Leeds, LS8 2EP
0113 269 3352
www.vintageinn.co.uk/restaurants/yorkshire/theroundhayfoxleeds

49. The Scarbrough Hotel, Bishopsgate Street

Named after a former owner (and not the resort, which has a different spelling), it stands on the site of a medieval manor house called Castle Hill that was rebuilt in 1765 as a most desirable residence. Henry Scarbrough bought the property in 1826, when it became known as The Kings Arms. In the late 1890s, Fred Wood established The Scarbrough Taps and named it after its first landlord, Henry Scarbrough. Wood also owned the City Varieties and the Queen's Theatre, Holbeck. He organised talent nights in the pub in the large concert hall and any act showing potential was put on at his City Varieties. Apart from being an enterprising pub owner and inspirational theatre owner, Wood was something of an innovator: he had shows from the Queen's Theatre relayed via cables to The Pack Horse and The Scarbrough so that drinkers could listen to the shows while they drank and if they came in at half time, they only paid half price. The image shows the dramatic masks of tragedy and comedy inn sign.

Others maintain that the name harks back to the Earl of Scarbrough, a title in the Peerage of England currently seated at Sandbeck Park near Rotherham and created in 1690 for Richard Lumley, 2nd Viscount Lumley, who is best remembered as one of the Immortal Seven who invited William of Orange to invade England and depose his father-in-law James II.

In a nice coincidence there is a Leeds Hotel in West Sandgate, Scarborough, and there was a Scarborough pub in Armley Road and the Scarborough Hotel in Scarborough Street.

Bishopsgate Street, Leeds, West Yorkshire, LS1 5DY
0113 243 4590
www.nicholsonspubs.co.uk/restaurants/yorkshireandthehumber/thescarbroughhotelbis hopsgatestreetleeds

The dramatic masks of tragedy and comedy inn sign.

Outside the Scarbrough.

50. The Ship Inn, Ship Inn Yard, Briggate

One of Leeds's oldest, there are records of its existence in the 1750s, when it was known as The Ship & Griffin. Appropriately, maritime paraphernalia decorates the walls. Ship Inn Yard runs between Lands Lane and Briggate. The pub was once popular with actors, musicians and other theatre people thanks to the nearby City Varieties, the Grand Theatre and the now demolished Empire and Theatre Royal.

No. 71 Briggate, Leeds, LS1 6LH
0113 246 8031
www.theshipleeds.co.uk
info@theshipleeds.co.uk

The Ship.

51. The Skyrack, St Michael's Road

The Skyrack is named after the local wapentake, which got its name from a large oak that grew for centuries in Headingley. Skyrack was one part of the wapentake – an Anglo-Saxon administrative meeting place – of the West Riding of Yorkshire. It was divided into upper and lower divisions. The lower division included the parishes of Aberford, Bardsey, Barwick-in-Elmet, Kippax, Thorner, Whitkirk and part of Harewood, while the upper division included the parishes of Adel, Bingley, Guiseley and parts of Harewood, Ilkley and Otley.

The Skyrack with its war memorial.

The word 'skyrack' comes from the Old English phrase '*scir ac*', meaning 'Shire Oak'. The tree finally collapsed in 1941, and there is a plaque to commemorate it on the garden wall of the Original Oak pub opposite.

No. 2 St Michael's Road, Leeds, LS6 3AW
0113 278 5836
www greeneking-pubs.co.uk

52. The Templar Hotel, Templar Street

The Templar from 1927 is commonly thought of as one of the few remaining 'traditional' corner pubs left in Leeds city centre. It has 'fine cream and green faience exterior' from former Leeds brewers Melbourne (*What Pub*). It is well worth a visit if only for the well-preserved Victorian booth back lounge that has some fine features and wood panelling, not to mention the displays charting the history of the Knights Templar. In the words of the *Yorkshire Evening Post*:

> With its ornate facade of Burmantofts tiles and its decorative wood-panelling inside, this is a fine example of the pub architect's art, a creation of utilitarian working class splendour in a city where too many others have been allowed to vanish. The Rising Sun in Kirkstall, the City of Mabgate behind Regent Street, the Beer Exchange in Woodhouse; each fine old drinking dens in their day, each wiped off the map in the name of progress… The Templar with its stained glass and tiled fireplaces, its elegant curving banquettes, still with the Bakelite bell-pushes which were once used to summon table service, its brass lanterns and oak beams, its lovely painted crockery and leaded lights.

No. 2 Templar Street, Leeds, LS2 7NU
0113 243 0318

The Templar Hotel.

53. The Three Hulats, Chapeltown

Once called the Mexborough Arms and the Bowling Green Inn in the early eighteenth century, it has been the Three Hulats since 1999. This is allegedly where the first Yorkshire cricket game was held in 1757. The cricket club here was one of three clubs, the others being bowling and Lascelles. A coaching inn, it was at the terminus junction of the Leeds-Harrogate turnpike road. Why the names? Chapel Allerton's historic connection with the Savile family, earls of Mexborough, is recalled in the Mexborough Arms. Their coat of arms includes three hulats or owls. At the time of writing Wetherspoon were apparently extending the Three Hulats into the former Foxes nightclub, which closed in the 1990s.

No. 3 Harrogate Road, Leeds, LS7 3NB
0113 262 0524
www.jdwetherspoon.com/pubs/all-pubs/england/west-yorkshire/the-three-hulats-leeds

54. The Three Legs, Three Legs Inn Yard, off Lower Headrow

This pub is famous for its Edwardian glazed façade. It started life around 1743 and still serves today. It was also known as the Three Kettle Spouts. Pubs with this name are usually found in the west (Wigan, Bolton, etc.), to welcome Manxmen. The legs signify kneeling to England, kicking Scotland and spurning Ireland.

The site is at the north-western end of Rockley Hall Yard, and was part of the Rockley Hall estate purchased by John Harrison from the Falkingham family around 1603. After Harrison's death in 1638 it was held in trust, until 1897 when it became the property of the Leeds Estate Company, who redeveloped much of Briggate, including the County Arcade between Briggate and Vicar Lane, at the rear of the Three Legs Inn.

The pub is pre-1743, when it was run by a William Mitton. In 1898 it was sold to a private owner, and in 1902 was bought by Tetley's, who undertook a major renovation between 1902 and 1914. The building also incorporated a shop. The façade was decorated with elaborate terracotta and glazed faience work. Inside, the bar came from the Marquis of Granby Inn on the north-east side of the Lower Head Row and demolished when the Headrow was widened in 1928.

No. 11 the Headrow, Leeds, LS1 6PU
0113 245 6316

Three Legs.

55. The Tommy Wass, Cleckheaton

In 1927 this Beeston pub was known as the Alice Doidge Refreshment Rooms, but the place dates from the late nineteenth century when it was a farmhouse on a 64-acre farm run by the eponymous Thomas Wass. Asa and Stephen Wass were the owners who lived nearby at Beech Cottage. The pub is named after their father, Thomas, who was born in 1832 in Morley. Thomas was the son of Stephen Wass, a wheelwright and carpenter from Easingwold. Thomas married Rachel Oades-Broadbent – a farmer's daughter – and they lived on a farm in Gipsy Lane, before moving into the building that's now the pub but was, at the time, a large farmhouse.

They had five daughters – Mary, Charlotte, Hephzibah, Annie and Amy – and three sons – Oliver, Asa and Stephen. Asa took over the farm after Thomas's death in 1887, followed by Stephen. The land on which the property was built was problematic: it belonged to the Church commissioners and there was a covenant imposed in the deeds to prevent the making, storage or sale of alcohol. Later, Bridge Farm, as it was called, due to its situation on the Dewsbury Road, became known as the Alice Doidge Refreshment Rooms when it was used as a changing room for the local church cricket and tennis clubs. After the death of Asa in 1924, the building was eventually purchased by Melbourne Brewery Company when the covenant was revoked.

As the farm had always been known locally as Tommy Wass's the family consented to the name when being used by the brewery when it opened as a pub in the late 1920s.

No. 450 Dewsbury Road, Leeds, LS11 7LJ
0113 450 0153
www.thetommywassleeds.co.uk

56. The Town Hall Tavern, Westgate

Opposite Leeds's Town Hall, built in 1926 and 'relaunched' in 2011, it was allegedly frequented by solicitors and police officers who would sit on one side of the pub preparing their cases for the nearby courts while the accused would make the most of their final moments of freedom on the other side. The pub had a fire alarm in the bar so that in the event of a fire any firemen who were in there having a swift half pint could be alerted. They were usually to be found in one of three places: the fire station, at home or in the pub, and there were alarms in all three.

The Town Hall Tavern.

Sadly, all this disappeared with the building of the new law courts on the site of the old Leeds fire station and the firemen's houses.

No. 17 Westgate, Leeds, LS1 2RA
0113 244 0765
www.townhalltavernleeds.co.uk

57. University Refrectory, University of Leeds

Live at Leeds is a live album by The Who. It was recorded at the University Refectory, University of Leeds, on 14 February 1970, and is the only live album that was released while the group were still actively recording and performing in their classic line-up of Roger Daltrey, Pete Townshend, John Entwistle and Keith Moon. It is probably the best live album of the times, after which is *Get Yer Ya-Yas Out* (September 1970) by the Rolling Stones.

Two shows were scheduled – one at the University of Leeds and the other at the University of Hull – to record and release a live album. The shows were performed on 14 February 1970 at Leeds and on 15 February at Hull, but technical problems with the recordings from the Hull concert (the bass guitar had not been recorded on some of the songs) made it inevitable that the Leeds show be released as the album. Townshend subsequently mixed the live tapes, intending to release a double album, but later chose to release just a single LP with six tracks:

Side one
'Young Man Blues' (Mose Allison), 4:46
'Substitute', 2:10
'Summertime Blues' (Jerry Capehart, Eddie Cochran), 3:22
'Shakin' All Over' (Johnny Kidd), 4:20

Side two
'My Generation', 14:45
'Magic Bus', 7.57

The *Live at Leeds* plaque.

58. The Victoria Family & Commercial Hotel, Great George Street

Behind the Town Hall, The Vic is TARDIS-like large and has a stunning interior replete with mahogany and etched glass. It had to be saved by the Leeds public from demolition in the 1970s.

Built by the Victoria Hotel Company in 1865, when, as the very grand sounding twenty-eight-bedroom Victoria Family & Commercial Hotel, it catered for those who had business at the Assizes Court in Leeds Town Hall, and for those visiting Leeds General Infirmary. This grand pub was connected to the Town Hall by an underground passage.

> I really envy anyone reading this who has never visited this beautiful, real ale paradise and still awaits the pleasure of stepping for the first time from the lobby into the long main room, with its long polished counter, brass details, floral tiles and gorgeous private booths. The back bar is simply a masterpiece; its engraved mirrors, ornate wooden carvings and stained glass would look perfectly at home in some High Anglican church. A big brass bell hangs in the doorway between the main bar and the snuggish Albert's Bar behind, and has been used no doubt to call time for generations.
>
> Simon Jenkins, *Yorkshire Evening Post*, 30 January 2014

The wonderful Victoria Hotel.

One of the bays.

Four years later:

> Its Sunday name remains in beautiful gilt lettering above the front door, and from Great George Street you enter a magnificent high-ceilinged lobby from where doorways lead to the Vic's three distinct drinking areas. The wooden panelling, gilt mirrors and ornate light fittings which have long marked this place out as different are all still there; Bridget's Bar to the left with its sumptuous décor and comfortable furnishing feels as welcoming as ever. Across the hallway is the main bar, whose etched glass and cosy booths offer that same familiar feel.
>
> Simon Jenkins, *Yorkshire Evening Post*, 13 December 2018

> lawyers still feel themselves called to the bar of this splendidly flamboyant gin palace to celebrate or commiserate after a case... It's easy to imagine them gossiping in the elaborately embellished mahogany booths that run along one side of the main lounge bar. Each booth offers comfortable leather seats, surrounded by decorative tiles and cut-glass mirrors. Stained glass gleams on the other side of an ornate bar.
>
> Chris Arnot, *The Telegraph*, 4 July 2008

No. 28 Great George Street, LS1 3DL
0113 245 1386

The bar in the Victoria.

59. West End House, Abbey Road

Close to Kirkstall Abbey and the museum, the West End House has been selling beer since 1867. The first licensee was William Tordoff, after whom a number of the streets in the vicinity are named. He was from a family of West Leeds licensees: his brothers Ben, Wilfred and Walter run pubs in Stanningley, Bramley and Armley respectively.

For many years the buildings were home to the headquarters of various Masonic lodges and societies between 1899 and 1922 when the pub changed its name to the West End Inn. The National Independent Order of Oddfellows, The Druids Lodge and the Steam Engine Workers Society all met there.

Local Kirkstall Brewery, which was then at the junction of Broad Lane and Wyther Lane and is now student accommodation, supplied beer to the pub between 1867 and 1936, and the pub displays much memorabilia from the brewery.

Kirkstall Abbey was founded in 1152 by Henry Lacy in woodland next to the River Aire 3 miles north-west of what was then Leeds village. It was a Cistercian foundation originating from Fountains Abbey and, like Rievaulx, Jervaulx and Fountains, became a powerful land owner, developing industries like iron forging, but, more significantly for the emergent Leeds, wool making. Kirkstall Abbey is said to have owned around 5,000 sheep at one time.

Kirkstall Brewery is synonymous in some ways with Kirkstall Abbey. Indeed, Yorkshire's first pub was the alehouse in which Samuel Ellis started brewing in 953 at Bardsey to the north of Leeds. It is still there under the guise once of the Priest's Inn and then of the Bingley Arms, but it is significant because of the Kirkstall Abbey monks who drank there on the way to St Mary's Abbey in York. Not only did they refresh themselves on their journeys but they brewed ale at the abbey itself – you might call this the first Kirkstall Brewery.

Kirkstall Brewery operated between 1833 and 1983 when it was closed by Whitbread. The brewery buildings have been well preserved and now provide accommodation for 1,000 or so Leeds Beckett University students at what is now Kirkstall Brewery Student Village. A new Kirkstall Brewery has been established nearby that has many echoes of the original: the old brewery crest, product names, and even their flagship 6 per cent beer, Dissolution Extra IPA, brewed from an original export beer from the 1860s.

A fascinating revelation was made during renovation of the buildings when it was discovered that a Second World War submarine engine was installed at the brewery as power back-up. This engine was one of a pair built in 1943 but was never actually installed in a submarine. The size of a Ford Transit van, it was sold in 1948 to the brewery and now resides at the Anson Engine Museum in Poynton, Cheshire.

No. 26 Abbey Road, Leeds, LS5 3HS
0113 278 6332
www.thewestendhouse.co.uk

60. Whitelock's Ale House, Turk's Head Yard

Grade II listed Whitelock's Ale House first opened its doors in 1715 as the Turk's Head in, fittingly enough, Turk's Head Yard. It is Leeds' oldest surviving pub.

In 1867 John Lupton Whitelock, an accomplished flautist with the Hallé and Leeds Symphony Orchestra, was granted the licence of the Turk's Head. The Whitelock family bought the pub in the 1880s and in 1886 completed a refurbishment that has left the marvellous décor we can still see today, including the long marble topped bar, etched mirrors and glass.

In the mid-1890s the pub was rebadged as Whitelock's First City Luncheon Bar and in 1897 John Lupton Whitelock installed electricity, including an exciting new revolving searchlight, at the Briggate entrance to the yard. Trick beer glasses in which a sovereign was placed ensured the punter got not the money but an electric shock.

Prince George (1902–42), later Duke of Kent, threw a party there in a curtained-off section of the restaurant. In those days a doorman ensured that men wore dinner jackets. Women were not allowed at the bar, so waiters served drinks to the women where they sat.

As noted the name Whitelock's derives from the family that used to own it, the first of whom was John Lupton Whitelock. Further on was Lupton Whitelock, an internationally renowned flautist who played for orchestras up and down the country. This led to the pub attracting

From when Whitelock's was the Turk's Head.

Whitelock's First City Luncheon Bar.

The Whitelock's interior then and now.

eminent musicians such as Sir John Barbirolli and Sir Malcolm Sergeant. It was also used by stage celebrities like Margot Fonteyn and Anna Neagle, and literary and artistic people such as John Betjeman and Jacob Kramer. The Leeds Savage Club met and drank here. Edmund Bogg, writer, rambler and bohemian, founded the club around 1891. When 'T'owd Chief' was not busy rambling or travelling around Yorkshire, armed to the teeth with sketch pads, pencils and notebooks rather than bows and arrows, he was hard at work penning one of his many excellent books on his beloved Yorkshire countryside, books for which he is still justly remembered today.

The Whitelock's exterior then and now.

Twins?

Leeds Savage Club, modelled on the Savage Club in London (founded in 1857 and still one of the leading bohemian gentlemen's clubs in London), brought together Leeds artists, musicians and writers in a bohemian, eccentric spirit as a refuge from the stiff and restricting everyday world. Membership was restricted to only fifty members who were called savages, with a chief as president, a scribe as secretary, and braves as committee men. The native Indian theme was Edmund Bogg's idea and he was duly elected chief, to preside in feathers and war-paint over the usually boisterous pow-wows in the wigwam, fuelled by firewater (whisky punch).

John Betjeman described Whitelock's as 'the Leeds equivalent of Fleet Street's Old Cheshire Cheese and far less self-conscious, and does a roaring trade. It is the very heart of Leeds.' It features in *Great Bars of the World*, rubbing shoulders with the Long Bar in Shanghai's Peace Hotel and Harry's in Venice. Whitelock's was sold to Scottish and Newcastle Breweries in 1944.

61. The White Swan, White Swan Yard

Cameron's White Swan is next door to the world-famous City Varieties Music Hall. Originally called the Swan Inn, the White Swan was built in 1762. City Varieties began life in 1760 when the White Swan Coaching Inn was built in a yard off Briggate, appropriately known as the White Swan Yard. The White Swan featured a singing room upstairs, where various acts, though not drama, were staged. Charles Thornton became the licensee of the White Swan in 1857 and, after refurbishment, reopened in 1865 as Thornton's New Music Hall and Fashionable Lounge, which was big enough to hold audiences of 2,000 or so. It remains a rare surviving example of Victorian era music halls of the 1850s and 1860s. A contemporary review says 'billiards and supper rooms were attached, and the place was noted for its attentive waiters'. A troupe of clog dancers was on the bill in 1897, one of which was Charlie Chaplin.

The refurbished White Swan has been embellished with playbills, dressing-room mirror lights behind the bar and a piano sits in the corner. Previous names have included The Piccadilly Bar in the 1970s, Barney's in the 1980s, The Blue Bar Cafe in the 1990s and even Bar Pacific in the 2000s. It traded as The Swan up to the closure of the City Varieties in 2009. The name Barney's comes from Barney Colehan, producer of the long-running BBC programme *The Good Old Days*, which was always filmed in the City Varieties.

No. 5 Swan Street, Leeds, LS1 6LG
0113 242 0187
www.whiteswanleeds.co.uk
info@whiteswanleeds.co.uk

62. The Wrens Hotel, New Briggate

The Wrens first opened in 1913 and, as it is on the opposite side of the road to the Grand Theatre, it was regularly frequented by the theatre's stars, staff and customers alike.

The Wrens has been refreshing thespians and their audiences since 1901. Originally built around 1838, it predates the theatre it would come to serve by forty years. It was an unnamed beerhouse run by a series of landlords until Alfred Edwin Wren took over and turned it into an eating house in the 1880s. It was renamed in 1901.

Other ornithological pubs flock to Yorkshire. They include The Phoenix near Barnsley (and York) and The Dotterel near Filey. The Eagle and Child (Conisborough and York) comes from the coat of arms of the earl of Derby while The Swan with Two Necks (Leeds and Wakefield) is a corruption of the Vintners Company crest – the swan with two nicks. Tadcaster has The Jackdaw, The Old Falcon and The Falcon. The Red Rooster is in Brighouse while Sheffield has its Pheasant. Ex birds are also represented: The Pigeon Pie is at Sherburn, is listed and dates from 1800. The Wrens in Leeds is a favourite with the Opera North crowd at the Grand Theatre nearby; despite the wrens on the sign, it has nothing to with the bird though – named as it is after Mrs Wren, the first landlord.

No. 61A New Briggate, Leeds, LS2 8JD
0113 2458888
info@thewrenshotel.co.uk

The Wrens Hotel.

Inside the Wrens today.

3

The Otley Run

The Otley Run is a world-famous pub crawl in Leeds that shares much in common with the Headingley Mile (also in LS6). The Otley Run is an obligatory rite of passage for students visiting or studying at Leeds, and there are lots of them, hailing from lofty places such as the University of Leeds, Leeds College of Music, Leeds Trinity University and Leeds Beckett University. Anyone not running the run is automatically awarded a third-class degree, with no honours whatsoever. The original Otley Run was enjoyed by farmers on market day who trundled into Leeds by tractor, stopping at all the pubs on the way. Guess what happened – nothing much has changed. Here are the sixteen lucky pubs involved today on the 1.5-mile stagger:

63. Woodies Craft Ale House

Woodies is *the* place to kick off.
No. 107 Otley Road, Headingley, Leeds, LS16 5JG

64. The Three Horseshoes

This is one of Headingley's oldest pubs.
No. 98 Otley Road, Headingley, Leeds, LS16 5JG

65. The New Inn

No. 68 Otley Road, Headingley, Leeds, LS6 4BA

'A butcher, a pig and a psychedelic gaggle of gals from 1969. With more and more stores offering fancy dress for hire, the streets of Headingley have become more and more Surreal' – as the Wikipedia caption would have it.

66. The Headingley Taps
Bennett Road, Headingley, Leeds, LS6 3HN

67. Manahattan
No. 19 Ash Road, Headingley, Leeds, LS6 3JJ

68. The Box
No. 8 Otley Road, Headingley, Leeds, LS6 2AD

69. The Skyrack
Nos 2–4 St Michael's Road, Headingley, Leeds, LS6 3AW

70. The Original Oak
No. 2 Otley Road, Headingley, Leeds, LS6 2DG

71. The Hyde Park
No. 2 Headingley Lane, Headingley, Leeds, LS6 2AS

72. The Library
No. 229 Woodhouse Lane, Leeds, LS2 3AP
If we insist on closing libraries then what better use to make of them than to repurpose them as pubs and therein drown our sorrows?

73. The Packhorse
No. 208 Woodhouse Lane, Leeds, LS2 9DX

74. The Eldon
No. 190 Woodhouse Lane, Leeds, LS2 9DX

75. Leeds University Union
The old bar or the terrace, or both.
Lifton Place, Leeds, LS2 9JZ

Above left: The Library – what better use for a redundant library?

Above right: Fun at the Fenton.

76. The Fenton

Nos 161–165 Woodhouse Lane, Leeds, LS2 3ED

77. Strawbs

Named after The Beatles' epic 'Strawberry Fields Forever': 'nothing is real' and 'living is easy with eyes closed' are quite apt lyrics, and it does have hallucinogenic 3D strawberries on the walls.
No. 159 Woodhouse Lane, Leeds, LS2 3ED

78. The Dry Dock

Woodhouse Lane, Leeds, LS2 3AX

The pub that's a boat. When you're sick here you're seasick.

Oak Inn.

4

Some Lost Leeds Pubs

'The destroying hand of progress.'

T. P. Cooper, *The Old Inns and Inn Signs of York*, 1897. Cooper was specifically referring to the wanton destruction of York pubs, but it applies just as much to the pubs of Leeds.

The Albion, Armley Road

Near Armley Gaol, this 1860s pub is world famous as the model for the trackside pub you would find in your Hornby 00 gauge model train set box. It was originally two shops, one of which became a beerhouse called The Fleece in 1873; the other became The Albion Hotel in 1886. Both

The Albion with its superb preserved sign.

were later bought by Peter Walker & Sons. After the First World War Leeds Council had a policy of refusing to renew licences to uneconomic pubs, and the Fleece and Albion were under threat, but were given a reprieve when they agreed to a merger instead. The name The Albion was chosen for the merged pub, which was sold to Tetley's in 1925. The pub, a designated heritage inn, was damaged by a blaze just six months after undergoing a £100,000 refit in 2009. Sadly, it has long since closed.

The Albion Hotel, Briggate

This Albion was built in 1824 and rebuilt in 1874 on the east side of Briggate at No. 142. The archway leads onto Albion Yard where there were stables and coach houses. It was all demolished to make way for Woolworth's, which opened on 1 December 1928, the second Woolworth's in Leeds.

Binks's Hotel, Rose and Crown Yard, Briggate

Also remembered as the Rose & Crown Hotel, this was a coaching inn in Rose and Crown Yard off Briggate looking towards Lands Lane in 1887. From 1783 the *Defiance* ran from here to Hull. The pub was demolished to make way for the Queen's Arcade in 1889. Lighted signs advertise for Binks's Bars No. 1 and 2 and billiard rooms. Binks's Hotel is named after the landlady, Maria Binks.

The Albion Hotel.

Binks's. Opposite is the Morley Dining Room, which offers ladies rooms, good beds, tobacco and cigars.

The Britannia Inn, Holbeck

Opened in 1901, it was acquired by Thomas Ramsden & Son Ltd in 1906. During one Feast Week on Holbeck Moor it sold a staggering 100 hogsheads of beer – 43,200 pints.

The Bull & Mouth Hotel, Briggate

Originally the Red Bear at No. 138 Briggate between Duncan Street and Kirkgate, this is one of Leeds' oldest hostelries. It was once a depot for heavy baggage wagons and was a coaching inn in 1800, soon to become one of the busiest such inns in Leeds with standing room for thirty horses in the cellar stables. The *Loyal Duncan* was the first coach to run from here, and the *True Briton* left from here every morning at 10 o'clock for Manchester, arriving at 6.30 in the evening.

The Bull & Mouth.

Bull & Mouth Hotel.

In 1903 it was renamed the Grand Central Hotel. In 1921 the name was changed again to the Victory Hotel, which closed in 1939 to make way for an extension to Woolworth's. The original name, as with the pre-Fire of London coaching house in London's Aldersgate Street and the pub in Horsham, derives from 'Boulogne Mouth', a reference to the town and harbour of Boulogne, as besieged by Henry VIII.

The Cemetery Tavern, Beckett Street

Built in the 1850s, it was not quite in the dead centre of town (the far end of the cemetery marked the north-east boundary of the township of Leeds) and not always a pub to die for. It was later renamed the more cheerful and hopeful Florence Nightingale but had to be demolished in 2008 when it was partly blown up by a gas explosion. The injured passers-by were taken to nearby St James.

The original House of Recovery or Fever Hospital was in Vicar Lane from 1802 to 1846. Leeds's earliest dispensary opened on 24 October in 1824 in the House of Recovery. When the House of Recovery moved to Beckett Street in 1846 the building was occupied by the Greyhound Inn, demolished in 1938. A 1904 poster in Water Street boasts of 'Beer by Electricity at the Greyhound Inn, Vicar Lane, Leeds'. The Fountain Head Inn was at No. 120 Beckett Street from at least 1872, owned by Melbourne Ales, then Hemingways, then Tetley's from 1960.

Cemetery Tavern was quite a common pub name. The Eldon in Woodhouse, and the Parnaby in Hunslet were both formerly called that.

The Chained Bull, Moortown

Bulls are everywhere in Yorkshire. Others include The Castle Howard Ox (York); The Blackwell Ox (Carlton and Sutton-on-the-Forest); The Wensleydale Heifer (West Witton); The Airedale Heifer (Mirfield) and The Craven Heifer (Heckmondwike, Ilkley, Stainforth, Barnoldswick and Skipton). Then there is The Bull and Mouth Hotel (above) in Briggate which was never really a bull but actually a red bear.

The Chained Bull (later The Bull) was a pub on Harrogate Road in Moortown. The first pub on the site was built in 1745 and replaced in 1925 by an Ind Coope house. This was demolished around 2008 after closure around 2006. It is now has the indignity of being part of the car park for Marks & Spencer's.

The City

This public house and restaurant is on Woodhouse Lane between Wormald Row and De Grey Street. An Albion Brewery pub.

City of Mabgate

Dating from 1857, the inn was converted to flats in 2006. Opposite was a cholera burial ground catering for the 1832 epidemic. The pub offered a fine example of world-famous Burmantofts faience with its green glaze tiling round the exterior.

Apparently there was a tunnel from the nearby parish church linking the Palace pub and the cellar of the Mabgate pub. This was allegedly built by the priests so they could visit prostitutes in secret and no doubt down a few pints at the same time. The Mabgate area of the city was a notorious red light district – the name 'Mab' was a slur in Shakespeare's day and beyond, meaning a prostitute. Queen Mab seems to be Shakespeare's invention as a title for a fairy queen as in *Romeo and Juliet* (1, 4, 53-58) – or quean, prostitute. The Black Bull was built on the site of Mabgate Hall (1673) and then rebuilt in 1868 as the Black Horse.

There was another Black Horse in Lawns Lane off Church Street, Hunslet, and the Brassmoulders also in Church Street. The White Horse was in Ward's Fold, Hunslet.

The City.

The Cobourg, Claypit Lane

A popular student pub at the turn of the millennium, with PlayStations, Ikea furniture and DJs playing through the night. It closed down in the early 2000s. After a brief time as Viva Cuba and Bar Red, it was a Scruffy Murphy's and later became a Japanese restaurant, closing for good in 2015. Cobourg is a town in Ontario, Canada, on Lake Ontario.

The Crown & Anchor, North Street

There are over 1,000 Crowns in the UK, so more than the 900 plus Red Lions. Crown often indicates a former crown property.

The Crown & Anchor.

The Crown Hotel, Crown Point Road

This establishment has been empty since the 1990s.

The Dock Green, Junction of Ashley Road and Stanley Road

The Dock Green, named of course after the famous police television soap, was built in 1903 at a cost of £6,408 as a police station house. It was sold in 1961 when it became the Dock Green and was opened by – who else? – Jack Warner, the actor who played George Dixon of Dock Green in the TV series. George Dixon made his debut in the film *The Blue Lamp* in 1950; at twenty-six minutes this was short-lived as he was shot by the villain played by Dirk Bogarde. Sent down for ever.

Ashley Road, Harehills, Leeds, LS9 7AB

The Dolphin Inn, No. 57–59 Vicar Lane

This pub has now been converted into shops.

The Duchess of York

This drinking hole was at No. 71 Vicar Lane, and was also known as the Robin Hood.

Above left: Dock Green pub sign – 'Evening all'.

Above right: The Robin Hood Inn.

The Duke William.

The Duke William, Bowman Lane

In 1890 Tetley's opened their first public house in Bowman Lane close to the brewery. The Duke William was shut in 1953 to become part of the yard of the brewery. It was demolished by Tetley's in 2002 – more cultural vandalism. 'Butcher' William Duke of Cumberland, on his victorious return from bloody Culloden, left a number of prisoners at York to show his gratitude for the city's hospitality. The Sheriff's chaplain read out the following message: 'And the Lord said unto Moses "Take all the heads of the people and hang them up before the sun".' Twenty-three were duly left to hang for ten minutes, stripped and quartered, their heads stuck on Micklegate Bar. Cumberland Street in York was named after the butcher duke.

The Duncan, The Headrow

The other Duncan, at No. 115 the Headrow, was, after the Whip, the second to last pub in Leeds to permit women through the door – in the early 1980s. However badly it failed when it came to gender politics, it could boast healthy human rights when it became the first pub in Leeds to ban smoking.

The Northern Monkey and Oxygen (clean, smoke-free air) Green Dragon (see below) and Guildford are previous names. Guildford dates back to the 1920s when this was in Guildford Street, before the Headrow was widened.

The Gamecock, Greenthorpe

This establishment could be found at the junction of Pudsey Road with Butt Lane (Gamble Hill).

The Golden Cock Inn, Nos 13–14 Kirkgate

Knocked down and replaced by a new Golden Cock.

Above left: The Gamecock Inn.

Above right: The old Golden Cock with its wonderful sign.

Hark to Rover, Kirkstall

There are numerous variants on the origin of this name. The Kirkstall Hark to Rover was in Morris Lane near Kirkstall Abbey. At the top of Abbey Walk is a house with the same name. Apparently, one night the abbey caught fire, but a dog's constant barking woke a monk who shouted the alarm 'Hark to Rover!' This roused the other monks, who extinguished the fire. Leodis tells us that the name comes from a local legend concerning a barmaid, Mary, who worked at the Star & Garter. She had taken a lover who was mixed up with a gang of highwaymen who had waylaid and killed a victim at Kirkstall Abbey. When she saw said lover burying the body, she fell to screaming and wailing in distress. Her dog, back in the cottage, heard her and began to bark incessantly. A poem by Robert Southey 'The Maid of the Inn' tells the tale. The Morris Lane Hark to Rover was replaced by another, in Spen Lane, nearby, which in turn closed in 2009.

The Star & Garter at Bramley carnival.

The Harp.

The Harp Tavern Concert Hall, Kirkgate

The Harp Tavern concert hall with the entrance to Coxon's Yard visible. London City & Midland Bank was on the left with James Waxworks on the right.

The Haunch of Venison, the Headrow and Lands Lane

The Haunch of Venison was on the south-east corner of the junction of the Headrow and Lands Lane. Jackson, in his 1889 guide, gives it as the site of Crosby House, built by the husband of Mrs Crosby, who attempted to help Charles I escape from Red Hall.

Horse & Jockey Hotel, No. 48 Commercial Street

Dating back to 1744, the Horse & Jockey was later replaced by the Mitre Hotel, which became a chocolate shop.

Jacob's Well, Meadow Lane

A Tetley House in 1964. References John 4: 12: 'whosover shall drinketh of this water shall thirst again.'

John of Gaunt

A pub named after the son of Edward III and father of Henry IV.

The Jubilee Hotel

This pub was situated at No. 165 the Headrow.

The Horse & Jockey.

The King Charles, Lands Lane

At the corner of Lands Lane with King Charles Croft, the King Charles was opened in 1845 and was a sad loss to Lands Lane when it was sacrificed in 1975 for Schofields. In the early 1970s, the Bradford & Bingley Building Society applied to Leeds Corporation to demolish the building to construct a new office block in its place. The council turned the application down since the pub was in a conservation area. There were historic links with Charles I, who was reputed to have been imprisoned in the Red Hall, which had once stood on the site.

Sadly, the then Minister of the Environment, Peter Shore, upheld an appeal by the Bradford & Bingley, and demolition work led to the downfall of the King Charles.

In the 1960s it was popular with mods along with Whitelock's, General Wade, and the Ostlers. There was a wood-panelled dining room upstairs, with 'old fashioned waitresses in black and white'.

The King Charles.

Cossins map of 1725 shows Red Hall to be at the junction of the Upper Head Row and Lands Lane. It was built in 1628, the first house in Leeds to be built of brick. During the civil war, in February 1646, Charles I was brought to Leeds as a prisoner. He was detained in a room, afterwards known as the King's Chamber, in Red Hall where he was visited by John Harrison, the Leeds benefactor and Royalist sympathiser, who brought the king a tankard of brown ale in which was secreted gold coins to facilitate an escape.

Mrs Crosby, a maid of Thomas Metcalf, is said to have offered the king women's clothes as a disguise in a bid to escape from Leeds. The king declined, but gave her his garter, saying that if his son (later Charles II) ever came to the throne she was to give the garter to him and tell him of how she came by it, and he would reward her. This Mrs Crosby did some time after 1660 and Charles II asked where she was from, and if she had a husband. She told him she was from Leeds and that her husband was a bailiff of the town. 'Then he shall be High Bailiff of Yorkshire' said the king. Crosby later built Crosby House, which stood on a site identified by Joseph Sprittles as a house on the Upper Headrow, which later became Arthur Cook's antique shop. Jackson in his 1889 guide gives it a different location – the Haunch of Venison pub at the corner of Land's Lane.

The King Edward

An establishment located at No. 18 King Edward Street that later became a bank.

The Leopard, Briggate

The Leopard was once a popular haunt of clothiers from Farsley. Daniel Defoe (1660–1731) describes the importance of pubs to the clothing industry in Leeds. He informs us that the cloth market was a swift, early morning affair starting at 7.00 a.m. and was all over by 9.00 a.m. when

The Leopard Hotel.

it was time for a good breakfast taken at public houses near the bridge. These meals were called Brig-End-Shots which, according to Ralph Thoresby 'the clothier may, together with his Pot of Ale, have a Noggin o' Pottage, and a Trencher of either Boil'd or Roast Beef for two Pence.'

The Malt Mill Inn

This was one of the public houses owned by Kirkstall Brewery in Broad Lane.

The Malt Shovel and the Unicorn Inn, Lowerhead Row

These two are over the road from each other in Lower Headrow or Lowerhead Row, as it was called then. On the left at No. 26 is the Malt Shovel mentioned in directories as far back as 1798. The inn was demolished when the Headrow was widened in 1928. At No. 31 is the Three Legs Inn and further down, The Vine. The Osborne Commercial Hotel is even further down on the left.

The Market Tavern or the Madhouse, Harewood Street and George Street

The Market Tavern near the Kirkgate Markets, on the corner of Harewood Street and George Street, won its nickname from the civil unrest that was a frequent occurrence in the pub. The photo is looking from Ludgate Hill. Apparently there was a one-armed bar steward worked there called Eli, who had a lot of girlfriends. A post on the internet states that it was 'not a place for the faint hearted, [late fifties] plenty of beer fuelled action here. There was a regular who had what looked like a thimble stuck on his nose, turned out someone bit the end of his hooter off in a scrap, it was recovered and sewn back on at the nearby Public Dispensary. I don't think the surgeon would have earned much in the tailoring trade!'

The Market 'Madhouse' Tavern.

Another theory for the nickname of the Madhouse is that it was adopted after a depressed customer hanged himself in the doorway of the pub. Another still maintains that it had problems with rats travelling over from the market. Since some of the customers would have kept ferrets to catch rabbits in local parks to go in the pot, when the rat problem got out of hand they would unleash the ferrets in the pub. The resulting mayhem gave rise to the 'madhouse' nickname.

The Marquis of Granby, No. 33 Eastgate

Famous for its huge curved bar, it was built in 1933 to replace an earlier eighteenth-century pub of the same name, but it shut down in 1984 and was converted into an office equipment shop, before closing again.

The Marquis of Lorne, Woodhouse Street

The Marquis of Lorne was at No. 121 Woodhouse Street. Later known as The Beer Exchange and before that Johnny Benns, it has now been converted to the inevitable flats. Otherwise known as Field Marshal John Campbell, 2nd Duke of Argyll, 1st Duke of Greenwich, KG, KT (1680–1743), styled Lord Lorne from 1680 to 1703, the marquis served in the Nine Years' War and fought during the War of the Spanish Succession under Marlborough. He became Commander-in-Chief in Scotland. During the Jacobite rebellion, he led the government army against the Jacobites.

McConnells, Briggate

Also known as the Alliance Vaults, this pub's seating was most often on barrels and the house specialty was Ind Coupe Old No. 2 Ale – only sold in halves. In the 1930s it was selling 3,000 pints of beer in a week, which was only one third of its turnover.

The Nelson Inn, Armley

Samuel Ledgard was landlord here from 1896 to 1952 (that's fifty-six years) when he was seventy-seven, as well as running the Angel Inn in Briggate and the Kings Arms in Tong, Bradford. A legend in his own tap room, he was father of eleven children from two marriages. He also owned a brewing and bottling plant behind the pub possibly making the Nelson the last home brew pub in Leeds. As if that wasn't enough he was the operator of Samuel Ledgard bus and coaches services in West Yorkshire, one of the biggest independent coach companies in the UK. He started with one vehicle in 1906, working at Yorkshire race meetings. From this he extended into general haulage, marquee rental, quarrying and farming – all from the pub. Until it closed the Samuel Ledgard Society held meetings in the pub. The brewing stopped when Samuel stopped.

The Old Cock & Bottle, Upperhead Row and Guildford Street

This was an eighteenth-century coaching inn on the junction of Upperhead Row (No. 18) and Guildford Street. In the 1830s the *Eclipse* ran to Ilkley every Monday, Wednesday, Friday and Sunday from the Cock & Bottle Inn. It was worked by Reuben Craven of the Woolpack Inn, Yeadon. *The Yorkshire Evening Post* names it as one of five theatrical pubs in Leeds, catering for the performers appearing at the Hippodrome, which was situated behind the pub in King Charles' Croft. By the 1930s the Cock & Bottle was hemmed in by the buildings of Schofields department store. In January 1938 the pub's owner retired. He sold the inn to Snowden Schofield, the owner of the store. The pub was absorbed into the store until 1961 when it was demolished when the new Schofields store was built. The licence of the Cock & Bottle was transferred to the New Eagle in York Road.

The Old Cock & Bottle, 1906.

The name refers to the tap used to draw ale and thus indicates a pub selling draught and bottled beer. Other pub-related establishments were the Hogshead, the Drop Inn at Guisely and the Local.

The Old George Commercial Hotel, Lower Briggate

Located on the east side of Lower Briggate, it closed in 1919. In 1791, it was advertised to be let as 'an ancient and well accustomed house, with stabling, vaults and other suitable conveniences'. Farrar Signs of Leeds are busy sign writing. The painted advertisement details 'Gentlemen's Smoking Concert Every Evening', and 'Splendid Home Brewed Ales'. Those single section ladders must have been a nightmare to transport and set up.

There was a Templar cross on the façade, indicating that it was originally owned by the Knights Templar or Hospitallers in the thirteenth century. This conferred certain privileges on the establishments that bore them, one being the 'Leeds Soke', an exemption from having to use the King's Mill in Swinegate to grind corn.

It opened in the seventeenth century as Ye Bush in the building shown above. The name was changed in 1714 to The George. The 'Old' was added around 1815 when the George and Dragon opened nearby. It was sometimes referred to as Simpsons Commercial Hotel after the Simpson family who ran it at the turn of the century. Celia Fiennes stayed here on her horseback journey round Britain. Charlotte Bronte once stayed there and drew on this in her illuminating description of the pub in *Jane Eyre*. It closed down around 1919 when the licence was not renewed and was demolished soon after. The owner then was a William J. Cudworth, a York Quaker who had inherited the pub, and with it a dilemma as he was obviously opposed to alcohol. He determined, however, that he would keep it open until the existing landlady, a Mrs Simpson, died.

The Old George.

The Old Kings Arms, Briggate

The Old Kings Arms was opposite the junction with Boar Lane. It was Leeds's earliest coaching inn. Originally it was the house of John Harrison (1579–1656), the seventeenth-century Leeds benefactor. When Harrison died it was converted into shops, and later became the King's Arms Tavern. Apart from serving ale and spirits it also was a meeting place for the trustees of the turnpike roads, and magistrates courts were held there.

On 19 May 1760 the first regular coach service between Leeds and London ran from the Old Kings Arms to the Swan with Two Necks in London. (Lad Lane, near the junction with Milk Street, Aldermanbury, and Cateaton Street. Lad Lane and Cateaton Street were among four streets amalgamated into Gresham Street in 1845.) The coaches were advertised as 'flying machines on steel springs', and the journey took four days. In 1785 the Leeds Royal Mail to London began operating from the Old Kings Arms, leaving Leeds at four in the morning and arriving in London at around 10.00 a.m. the next day, the journey taking around thirty hours. In 1813 the Old Kings Arms closed as an inn, but was used as the offices of the *Leeds Mercury* until it was demolished when Duncan Street was widened in 1904.

The Old Kings Arms is famous for the siege here in 1753. The good people of Leeds were rebelling against the turnpike charges and attacked the toll gates at Harewood Bridge but were repulsed; soldiers were called up to guard the turnpikes. Three men were arrested for non-payment and imprisoned and taken to the Old Kings Arms to stand trial. The rioters pelted the inn and the soldiers guarding it. Their response was to open fire, initially using powder but then live rounds. Eight rioters were shot dead and forty injured, some of whom died later.

The Old Nags Head Hotel

This pub was on Kirkgate opposite Leeds parish church.

The Old Nags Head.

The Old Travellers Rest, Bramley.

The Old Travellers Rest, Bramley

The Old White Swan Inn, Swan Street

Charles Thornton (1820–81) owned the Old White Swan Inn in Swan Street, and was the proprietor of the Varieties Music Hall (now the Leeds City Varieties). In 1873 he built a block of shops and offices, Thornton's Buildings, where the Upper Headrow meets with Lands Lane. In 1875 Thornton sought permission to demolish the Old Talbot Inn on Briggate, to build a new arcade of shops on the site. The Talbot was not just any old pub; it was one of the oldest inns in Leeds and boasted the finest frescoes on the walls in a room there. The inn was a venue for cockfighting, and in the seventeenth century it was where the circuit judges stayed while in Leeds.

The Ostlers, Trinity Street

The Ostler was the man employed to look after the horses of people staying at an inn.

The Owl Inn, Rodley Lane

The Owl inn reflected the owl on the city arms of Leeds, so a sad loss to the city. There are three owls on Leeds City Council's coat of arms, huge golden owl statues outside Civic Hall and sculptures and paintings of owls at twenty-four other locations around the city.

The Peel, Boar Lane

The pub changed its name from The Peel Hotel in 1976 to the Square on the Lane. It had the longest bar in Leeds when it was The Peel. The bar itself was sold on to a pub named Le Chateau, in Cork, Ireland. From the *Secret Leeds* website:

Post by Rusty, Wednesday 09 June 2010, 5:14 p.m.:

My name is Shane and I used to work downstairs in the Peel with Bob on the back door. We'd have to mop about two inches of standing water from a leaking road-drain, before we could open up. I'm sure Health & Safety would've closed the place in a flash. A guy called Mick, and his chick Sharon used to collect glasses. Barbara or Betty used to run the decks, they also did a similar disco on Tuesdays in the Cemetry opposite St James hospital. A pint of Websters' Best was 17p!!! 20 Players' No. 6 were 21p, you could have a great night out for less than £10 and then off to the WigWam in the Merrion Centre, where I met the lost love of my life, a wonderful girl called Kathryn Ball (Sandy) from Horsforth.

Post by Precinct Boy, Friday 11 June 2010, 12:23 a.m.:

Was Mick the glass collector the same guy who use to crunch glass in his mouth and swallow it, he also used to empty ashtrays into a pint and down it in one.

Wow!

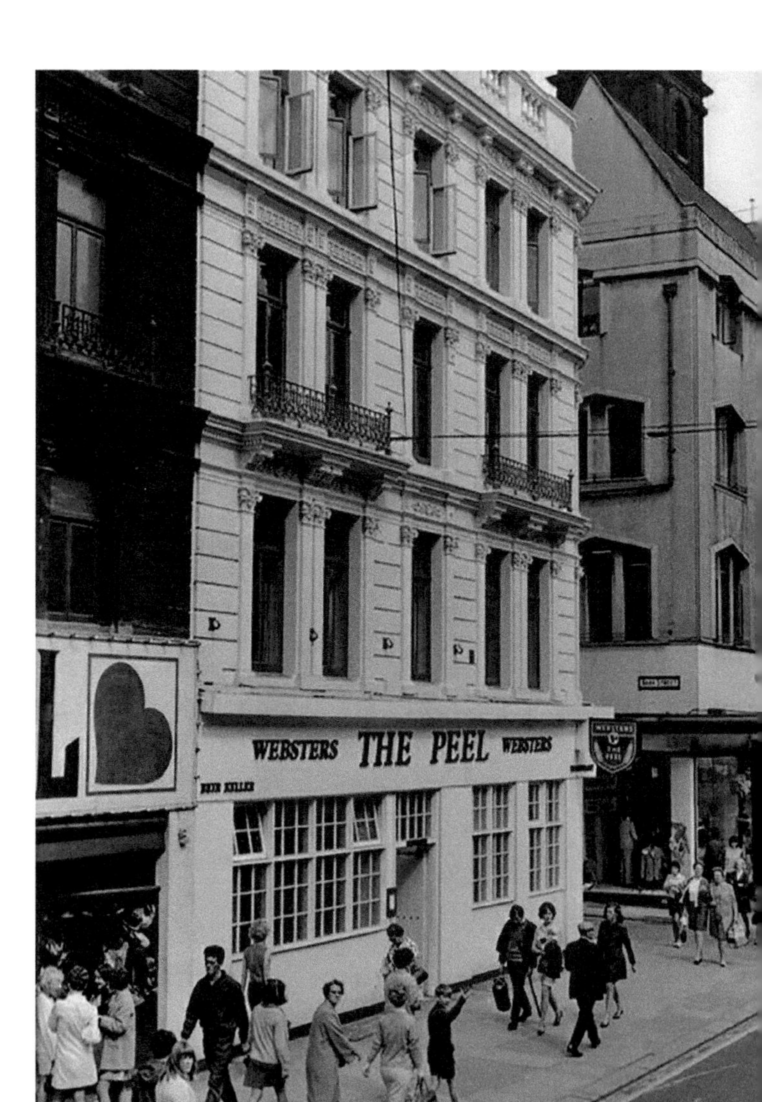

The Peel.

The Phoenix Inn, No. 46a Kirkgate

This inn opened in the early 1830s and was demolished around 1866 to make way for the railway bridge that crossed Kirkgate.

The Pineapple Inn (Hunslet)

This inn was first recorded in the High Street, or Pottery Fields, in 1871. There were four Pineapples or Pine-apples in Leeds at one time – another was in Accommodation Road, Burmentofts. Apparently, of the four Leeds pubs with that name – No. 77 Accommodation Road, Nos 167–169 Park Lane, No. 4 Ivory Street, High Street, Quarry Hill – only Ivory Street is ever shown as the Pineapple (all one word). There is an old pub near Heath Common in Wakefield called the Pineapple. In the 1700s a pineapple on the gatepost was a sign that a sailor was home from overseas (welcome home!), which possibly accounts for the unusual pub name. On the other hand, pinecones used to be called pineapples...

Other pubs in Pottery Fields are said to have included Union Inn (onion?) and, to keep up the fruit and veg link, the Cabbage Inn.

The Punch Clock, Low Road, Hunslet

Named after the clocking-in time machine, the Punch Clock later revived as the Crooked Clock after being taken over by the former landlord of the Crooked Billet nearby (also closed) on the opposite side of the road. This pub is renowned for the drinking contest it held between workers of the Yorkshire Copper Works and Coghlan's Forge. Nearby too was the Old Red Lion. The name is not quite as quintessentially English as many people think. The emblem on the ubiquitous (Old) Red Lions often originates from the time of James I and VI of Scotland (1566–1625). James ordered that the heraldic red lion of Scotland be displayed on all buildings of importance and that included pubs. Other Red Lions may be named after the heraldry of local nobles or after John of Gaunt, whose personal badge was such a beast.

The Rising Sun, No. 290 Kirkstall Road

Once magnificent nineteenth-century pub turned into a furniture shop in 2011 and gutted by fire in 2013. The pub was bought by Tetley's in 1923, selling at the time twenty-four hogsheads a week – 10,368 pints. In 1936 sales fell to nineteen hogsheads, then increased in 1941 to twenty-two. To keep up the astronomical theme, the Morning Star was at 182 Kirkstall Road, demolished in the 1960s.

The Robin Hood, No. 71 Vicar Lane

The Robin Hood Hotel had a bad reputation in Victorian times as being the haunt of pimps and prostitutes. More recently the name changed to the Duchess of York and it became a popular music venue until its closure in 2000.

The Roscoe Inn, Chapeltown Road

The Irish-inflected Roscoe opened in 1857 and was demolished in 1983. Leeds's last beerhouse could only sell wines and spirits when its licence was amended in 1976.

The Rose & Crown, Briggate

Another important Leeds coaching inn famous for its cockpit and cockfights, which were regularly advertised in the *Leeds Intelligencer*.

The *Defiance* ran from here to Hull in 1783, and the *Diligence* to Liverpool, But the most lucrative were the mail coaches for York, Sheffield, Scarborough, Manchester and Liverpool.

Robin Hood Inn.

The Rose & Crown hit the headlines in November 1831 when a package was put on the Edinburgh coach and was seized by police. It was addressed to Mr Ben Thomson, Mail Office, Edinburgh, and contained the body of Robert Hudson, which had been exhumed by bodysnatchers from the churchyard at East Ardsley. They were sending it to a surgeon in Edinburgh for use at the medical school there. The inn was demolished in 1888–89 and the Queen's Arcade was built on the site.

The Royal Hotel, Lower Briggate

In 1692, when this pub was first built, it was called the New King's Arms. It boasted roomy and well-ventilated stables for eighteen horses. The first coaches ran from 1765, and in 1834 when Royal Mail coaches came on board the name was changed to the Royal Hotel. The opening of the North Midland Railway in 1840 saw the end of the mail coaches.

When it was decided to demolish the Royal Hotel to build flats, it was also decided that the façade should be retained. However, during demolition the façade collapsed, leaving the developers in a quandary: should they rebuild the expensive frontage? A fibreglass representation of the façade was made and this is what you see today.

The Royal with its stunning façade.

The Skinners Arms, Buslinghtorpe

This Skinners was built in the 1920s to replace the pub over the road, which had been there since around 1800. Its name reflects the local leather and tanning industry. It was also known as T'Treacle Pot. It closed in 2008.

The Star & Garter Inn, Bridge Road

Bar-Celona was formerly the Star & Garter Inn, where actress Sarah Siddons was said to have stayed while playing at the Leeds Theatre in Hunslet in 1807. She will not have been welcomed back as her parting shot after performing there was 'Farewell ye brutes, and forever, I trust; ye shall never torture me again!'

The name of the pub comes from the Order of the Garter, of which the star is part. Built in the eighteenth century, it was a former stagecoach inn at the mill race at the junction of the old Leeds-Bradford (1734) and Leeds-Kendal (1753) turnpike roads. In the nineteenth century it was a meeting and trading place for local woollen manufacturers. After its time as a pub it was relegated to an amusement arcade.

St James's Tavern

Located at No. 74a St James Street, the Oxford Hand Laundry is at No. 72.

St James's Tavern.

The Victoria. Waiting for opening time?

The Victoria, York Road

Now a pet shop.

The Whip Inn, off Duncan Street

The Whip dates back to around 1830 and was built on one of the old Briggate burgage plots. The Whip Inn (now Mook) could be found at Nos 3 and 5 Hirst's Yard off Duncan Street. It owes its name to its days as an old nineteenth-century coaching inn. In the 1930s, it sold more beer than any other pub in Leeds: at its height 25,000 pints of beer a week were sold to a male-only clientele. It wasn't until the 1970s that ladies' toilets were built to comply with the law. Women were not allowed in until the early 1980s, making it the last men-only drinking house in Leeds.

The Whip.

The Duncan, the Headrow

This pub was the penultimate bastion of male consumption. In 1975 workmen carrying out tests on a nearby building accidentally broke through some panelling beneath a staircase and found a huge arched cavern, which had obviously been used as stables. Wooden troughs were still on the walls. In 1994, it was renamed the Fiddler's Elbow by Tetley's, who owned it at the time, but it was renamed the Whip after objections by the Leeds Civic Trust.

The White Hart Inn, White Hart Yard, Briggate

The yard and inn were demolished to make way for the County Arcade between 1898 and 1903.

The White Hart.

William IV Inn, Briggate

Originally the Elephant Inn in Elephant Yard, the name was changed in deference to the king.

The William the Fourth.

The White Swan, Well Lane, Chapeltown

The White Swan's licence was revoked in 1867, presumably for rowdy behaviour and other shenanigans. It then turned over a new leaf – some would say that it went a bit too far – and became a temperance pub. It is one of the first British Workman's pubs. A sign read: 'British Workman's Public Houses – A Public House without the drink, where may read, and smoke and think Then sober home return; a stepping stone this house you'll find, Come leave your rum and beer behind And truer pleasures learn.' Beverages included Winterine, a temperance wine, Anti-Burton, an alcohol-free beer, and aerated milk champagne.

THE BRITISH WORKMAN

BETTER DO IT AT ONCE.

SUNDAY WORK.

CONTENTMENT.

PRIZES for WORKING MEN.

A page from the *British Workman*.

A temperance coffee cart.

Temperance.

The Woolpack Inn, Durham Street

The Woolpack Inn stopped being a pub in the late 1950s, although the building remained. The Woolpack was another of those pubs whose licence was surrendered to facilitate the opening of other pubs. Along with the Somerby Inn, Somerby Street, and the Springhill Tavern, Buslingthorpe Lane, they all surrendered their licences for the Halton Moor Hotel.

Some Other Lost Pubs

The Black Dog, Ellerby Lane
The Castleton, Armley Road
The Hogshead, Albion Street
The Scarborough Arms, Armley Road
The Scotsman, Kirkgate
Skew Bridge Hotel, No. 19 Gelderd Road

Leeds's Nine Coaching Inns

The Old Kings Arms
The Hotel Inn (later the Royal Hotel)
The Golden Lion
The Bull and Mouth
The Albion
The Talbot
The Rose & Crown
The White Horse
The Star & Garter

5

Closing Time

'It'll all end in beers'

Anon

'Now – Will someone take me to a pub?'

G. K. Chesterton (1874–1936)

'The Landlord' by F. W. Elwell (1870–1958), in Ferens Art Gallery, Hull.

About the Author

Paul Chrystal has degrees from the universities of Hull and Southampton. He went into medical publishing for thirty or so years but now combines this with writing features for national newspapers and history magazines. He has appeared regularly on BBC local radio, on the BBC World Service and Radio 4's p.m. programme. In 2018 Paul contributed to a six-part series for BBC2, 'celebrating the history of some of Britain's most iconic craft industries', in this case chocolate in York. He has contributed to a Channel 5 programme on chocolate brands, which aired in 2019. He has been history advisor for a number of York tourist attractions and is the author of 100 or so books on a wide range of subjects, including *Central Leeds Through Time*, *Leeds in 50 Buildings*, *Leeds's Military Legacy*, *A–Z of Leeds* and *Old Bramley & Stanningley*, which is in press. He is a regular reviewer for and contributor to *Classics for All* and a contributor to the Classics section of OUP's Oxford Bibliographies Online. He is editor of *York Historian*, the journal of the Yorkshire Architectural & York Archaeological Society. Also, Paul is guest speaker for the prestigious Vassar College New York's London Programme in association with Goldsmith University. Paul lives near York and is married with three (grown-up) children.

By the same author:
Central Leeds Through Time
Leeds in 50 Buildings
Leeds's Military Legacy
A–Z of Leeds
Old Bramley & Stanningley (in press)
Hull Pubs
Pubs In & Around York
Pubs in the Yorkshire Dales
Harrogate Pubs (including Knaresborough)
Place Names of Yorkshire (including pub names)
Yorkshire Murders, Manslaughter & Madness